Powering the Future A Guide to Sustainable Energy Systems for Everyone

Florian

Copyright © [2023]

Author: Florian

Title: Powering the Future A Guide to Sustainable Energy Systems for Everyone

All rights reserved. No part of this publication may be reproduced or transmitted in any form or by any means, electronic or mechanical, including photocopying, recording, or any information storage and retrieval system, without prior written permission from the author.

This book is a self-published work by the author Florian

ISBN:

TABLE OF CONTENTS

Chapter 1: Introduction to Sustainable Energy Systems — 07

The Importance of Sustainable Energy

What Are Sustainable Energy Systems?

Benefits of Adopting Sustainable Energy Systems

Challenges and Barriers to Sustainable Energy Adoption

Chapter 2: Understanding Renewable Energy Sources — 15

Solar Energy

Wind Energy

Hydropower

Geothermal Energy

Biomass Energy

Chapter 3: Harnessing Solar Energy — 25

Photovoltaic Systems

Solar Thermal Systems

Concentrated Solar Power (CSP)

Solar Energy Storage and Grid Integration

Chapter 4: Utilizing Wind Power 33

Wind Turbines and Wind Farms

Offshore Wind Energy

Wind Energy Storage and Grid Integration

Chapter 5: Tapping into Hydropower Resources 39

Run-of-River Hydropower

Reservoir Hydropower

Pumped Storage Hydropower

Small-Scale Hydropower

Chapter 6: Exploring Geothermal Energy 48

Geothermal Power Plants

Direct Use of Geothermal Energy

Geothermal Heat Pumps

Enhanced Geothermal Systems (EGS)

Chapter 7: Utilizing Biomass for Energy Production 56

Bioenergy Conversion Technologies

Biomass Power Plants

Biogas and Anaerobic Digestion

Biofuels for Transportation

Chapter 8: Integrating Sustainable Energy Systems into Buildings 64

Energy-Efficient Design Principles

Passive Solar Design

Net-Zero Energy Buildings

Smart Grid Technologies for Buildings

Chapter 9: Sustainable Energy for Transportation 73

Electric Vehicles and Charging Infrastructure

Hydrogen Fuel Cell Vehicles

Biofuels and Sustainable Aviation Fuels

Public Transportation and Sustainable Mobility

Chapter 10: Policies and Incentives for Sustainable Energy Adoption 81

Government Initiatives and Regulatory Frameworks

Financial Incentives and Subsidies

International Cooperation for Sustainable Energy Transition

Chapter 11: Overcoming Challenges and Ensuring a Sustainable Future 87

Energy Storage Technologies and Solutions

Grid Modernization and Resilience

Energy Education and Awareness

Collaborative Efforts for Sustainable Energy Development

Chapter 12: The Role of Individuals in Powering the Future   96

Energy Conservation and Efficiency Measures

Consumer Choices for Sustainable Energy

Community-Based Energy Projects

Empowering Individuals to Drive Change

Conclusion: Embracing Sustainable Energy Systems for a Brighter Future   104

Chapter 1: Introduction to Sustainable Energy Systems

The Importance of Sustainable Energy

In today's rapidly changing world, the significance of sustainable energy cannot be emphasized enough. As our dependence on fossil fuels continues to contribute to climate change and other environmental issues, it has become imperative to shift towards sustainable energy systems. This subchapter will delve into the crucial reasons why sustainable energy is essential for everyone, with a particular focus on its significance in the field of environmental engineering.

First and foremost, sustainable energy sources such as solar, wind, hydro, and geothermal power are renewable and inexhaustible. Unlike fossil fuels, which are finite resources, sustainable energy can be harnessed indefinitely without depleting the Earth's resources. This aspect alone makes sustainable energy a viable long-term solution to our energy needs.

One of the most pressing concerns of our time is climate change. The burning of fossil fuels releases greenhouse gases into the atmosphere, leading to a rise in global temperatures and extreme weather events. By transitioning to sustainable energy, we can significantly reduce our carbon footprint and mitigate the impacts of climate change. Environmental engineers play a vital role in this transition by developing innovative technologies and systems that harness sustainable energy efficiently.

Furthermore, sustainable energy sources have a minimal impact on the environment compared to traditional energy sources. For instance, solar and wind power do not produce harmful emissions or pollution during their operation. This reduction in pollution has numerous health benefits, including lower rates of respiratory diseases and improved air quality. Environmental engineers, with their expertise in sustainable energy systems, can help design and implement these technologies to minimize the negative environmental impacts.

In addition to environmental benefits, sustainable energy also offers economic advantages. Investing in renewable energy technologies can create jobs, stimulate economic growth, and reduce reliance on imported energy sources. As the world's population continues to grow, sustainable energy systems provide a stable and secure energy supply that is not subject to geopolitical conflicts or price fluctuations.

Overall, the importance of sustainable energy cannot be overstated. Its role in mitigating climate change, preserving the environment, improving public health, and fostering economic growth is critical. Environmental engineers have a significant role to play in advancing sustainable energy systems and ensuring a sustainable future for everyone. By embracing sustainable energy, we can power the future in an environmentally-friendly and economically viable manner.

What Are Sustainable Energy Systems?

In today's rapidly evolving world, the need for sustainable energy systems has become more critical than ever before. As we face the challenges of climate change and dwindling fossil fuel resources, it is imperative that we find alternative energy solutions that are environmentally friendly and capable of meeting our energy demands in the long term. This subchapter aims to shed light on what sustainable energy systems are and their significance in addressing the global energy crisis.

Sustainable energy systems are those that harness renewable sources of energy, such as solar, wind, hydro, geothermal, and biomass, to generate power. Unlike conventional energy systems that rely heavily on fossil fuels, which release harmful greenhouse gases during combustion, sustainable energy systems have minimal or zero carbon emissions. This makes them an ideal choice for mitigating climate change and reducing our carbon footprint.

One of the primary benefits of sustainable energy systems is their ability to provide a constant and reliable source of energy. Renewable sources, such as solar and wind, are abundant and widely available, ensuring a continuous supply of power. Additionally, these systems are less vulnerable to price fluctuations compared to fossil fuels, making them economically advantageous in the long run.

Moreover, sustainable energy systems offer a wide range of environmental, social, and economic benefits. By reducing our reliance on finite fossil fuels, we can improve air quality, preserve ecosystems, and mitigate the adverse effects of climate change. Furthermore, the development and implementation of sustainable energy systems create job opportunities and stimulate economic growth, especially in the field of environmental engineering.

Environmental engineering plays a crucial role in designing, developing, and implementing sustainable energy systems. Professionals in this niche are at the forefront of finding innovative ways to harness renewable energy sources efficiently and effectively. Their expertise is vital in ensuring that sustainable energy projects are economically viable, environmentally sound, and socially acceptable.

In conclusion, sustainable energy systems are the future of energy production. They offer numerous benefits, including reduced carbon emissions, reliable energy supply, and positive economic impacts. Environmental engineering plays a pivotal role in driving the development and implementation of these systems. As we strive to create a sustainable future, understanding and embracing sustainable energy systems is essential for everyone, regardless of their background or profession. By working together, we can power the future with clean and renewable energy, ensuring a healthier planet for generations to come.

Benefits of Adopting Sustainable Energy Systems

In recent years, the world has witnessed a growing awareness of the urgent need to transition from conventional energy sources to sustainable energy systems. As we face the challenges of climate change and depletion of finite resources, adopting sustainable energy systems has become imperative. In this subchapter, we will explore the numerous benefits that come with embracing sustainable energy.

1. Environmental Benefits: One of the most significant advantages of sustainable energy systems is their minimal impact on the environment. Unlike fossil fuels, sustainable energy sources such as solar, wind, and hydroelectric power do not produce harmful greenhouse gas emissions. By reducing our reliance on fossil fuels, we can mitigate climate change, improve air quality, and protect ecosystems.

2. Energy Security: Sustainable energy systems offer a more stable and secure energy supply. Unlike fossil fuels, which are subject to price volatility and geopolitical tensions, renewable energy sources are abundant and widely available. By diversifying our energy mix, we reduce dependence on foreign oil and enhance energy independence.

3. Economic Growth: Adopting sustainable energy systems drives economic growth and job creation. The renewable energy sector has seen significant expansion and investment, leading to the creation of numerous job opportunities. Additionally, transitioning to sustainable energy systems can reduce energy costs, leading to long-term savings for consumers and businesses.

4. Improved Public Health: The use of sustainable energy systems can have a positive impact on public health. Traditional energy sources,

such as coal and oil, release pollutants that contribute to respiratory diseases and other health issues. By transitioning to cleaner energy sources, we can reduce pollution and improve overall public health.

5. Technological Innovation: Embracing sustainable energy systems spurs technological innovation. As we invest in renewable energy research and development, new technologies and breakthroughs emerge. This not only enhances our energy systems but also drives advancements in other industries, fostering economic growth and promoting a sustainable future.

6. Community Resilience: Sustainable energy systems empower communities to become more resilient in the face of natural disasters and emergencies. Distributed renewable energy generation, such as solar panels on rooftops, can provide electricity during power outages, ensuring crucial services like hospitals, schools, and emergency response centers remain operational.

In conclusion, adopting sustainable energy systems offers a multitude of benefits for both the environment and society as a whole. From mitigating climate change and improving public health to driving economic growth and technological innovation, transitioning to sustainable energy is a crucial step towards a more sustainable future. By embracing these benefits and making conscious choices, we can all contribute to a cleaner, more secure, and resilient world for future generations.

Challenges and Barriers to Sustainable Energy Adoption

Introduction:

As the world faces the growing threat of climate change, the need for sustainable energy systems has become increasingly urgent. However, the adoption of sustainable energy technologies is not without its challenges and barriers. This subchapter will explore some of the key obstacles that hinder the widespread adoption of sustainable energy solutions, with a focus on the perspective of environmental engineering.

1. Cost and Affordability:
One of the major challenges to sustainable energy adoption is the initial investment required. Many renewable energy technologies, such as solar panels or wind turbines, have higher upfront costs compared to traditional fossil fuel-based systems. This cost barrier can be particularly challenging for individuals or communities with limited financial resources. Additionally, the cost of energy storage and grid integration can also pose significant challenges in the transition to sustainable energy systems.

2. Infrastructure and Grid Limitations:
The existing energy infrastructure, designed primarily for centralized fossil fuel-based power generation, may not be suitable for accommodating the decentralized nature of sustainable energy sources. Integrating renewable energy into the grid presents technical challenges, including intermittency, fluctuating power generation, and voltage control. Upgrading and expanding the grid infrastructure to support sustainable energy sources can be a complex and costly process.

3. Policy and Regulatory Frameworks: Inadequate policy and regulatory frameworks can hinder the adoption of sustainable energy systems. Uncertain government policies and inconsistent incentives can discourage investments in renewable energy projects. Additionally, complex permitting processes and bureaucratic barriers can slow down the implementation of sustainable energy projects, making it harder for individuals and communities to transition to cleaner energy sources.

4. Public Awareness and Perception: Limited public awareness and misconceptions about sustainable energy can also act as barriers to adoption. Many people are still unaware of the environmental benefits and long-term cost savings associated with sustainable energy systems. Education and awareness campaigns are essential to debunking myths and promoting the advantages of renewable energy, encouraging individuals and communities to embrace sustainable energy solutions.

Conclusion:

While the transition to sustainable energy systems is crucial for mitigating climate change and securing a cleaner future, it is not without its challenges. Overcoming barriers such as cost, infrastructure limitations, policy frameworks, and public perception will require concerted efforts from both environmental engineering professionals and society as a whole. By addressing these challenges head-on, we can pave the way for a sustainable energy future that benefits not only the environment but also our economy and quality of life.

Chapter 2: Understanding Renewable Energy Sources

Solar Energy

Solar energy is a vital and powerful source of sustainable energy that has the potential to revolutionize the way we power our future. In this subchapter, we will explore the incredible potential of solar energy and its importance in sustainable energy systems for everyone.

Solar energy is derived from the sun, which emits an enormous amount of energy. This energy can be harnessed and converted into electricity or used directly for heating or lighting purposes. Solar power is clean, renewable, and abundant, making it a key player in reducing our dependence on fossil fuels and combating climate change.

The utilization of solar energy offers numerous benefits, especially in the field of environmental engineering. One of the most significant advantages is that solar power does not produce harmful emissions, such as greenhouse gases or air pollutants. This makes it a perfect alternative to conventional energy sources that contribute to global warming and air pollution.

Another advantage of solar energy is its versatility. Solar panels can be installed on rooftops, in open spaces, or even integrated into building materials such as windows and facades. This flexibility allows for the integration of solar power systems into existing infrastructure without compromising aesthetics or functionality. Additionally, solar energy systems can be scaled up or down to meet the specific needs of individuals, communities, or large-scale industrial operations.

Moreover, solar energy is a decentralized and independent source of power. By generating electricity on-site, solar energy reduces the need for long-distance transmission lines, minimizing energy losses during transmission. This aspect is particularly relevant in remote areas or developing countries that lack access to reliable electricity grids.

Furthermore, solar energy can provide economic benefits to individuals and communities. Solar panels not only reduce electricity bills but can also generate excess electricity that can be sold back to the grid, creating a source of income. Additionally, the installation and maintenance of solar power systems create job opportunities in the renewable energy sector, boosting local economies.

In conclusion, solar energy is a game-changer in the field of sustainable energy systems. Its clean and renewable nature, coupled with its versatility and economic benefits, make it an essential component of our future energy landscape. Whether you are an environmental engineer or simply an individual interested in sustainable living, embracing solar energy is a step towards a greener and more sustainable future for everyone.

Wind Energy

Wind energy is one of the most promising and rapidly growing sources of renewable energy in the world today. Harnessing the power of the wind to generate electricity has numerous environmental and economic benefits, making it a key component of sustainable energy systems. In this subchapter, we will explore the potential of wind energy and its role in addressing the global energy crisis.

Wind energy is derived from the natural movement of air masses caused by temperature and pressure differences in the Earth's atmosphere. By using wind turbines, we can convert the kinetic energy of the wind into electrical energy. These turbines consist of large, rotating blades that capture the wind's energy, which is then converted into electricity through an internal generator.

One of the main advantages of wind energy is its renewable nature. Unlike fossil fuels, which are finite resources, wind is an abundant and inexhaustible source of energy. With proper infrastructure and technological advancements, wind energy has the potential to meet a significant portion of our global electricity demand.

Wind energy also offers a clean and sustainable alternative to traditional energy sources. Unlike coal or natural gas power plants, wind turbines produce no greenhouse gas emissions or air pollutants during operation. This makes wind energy vital in mitigating climate change and reducing our carbon footprint.

Furthermore, wind energy projects create job opportunities and stimulate economic growth. The wind power industry requires skilled technicians, engineers, and manufacturers, contributing to local and national employment rates. Additionally, wind farms can provide a stable source of income for landowners who lease their land for turbine installation.

In recent years, there have been significant advancements in wind turbine technology, resulting in increased efficiency and reduced costs. Offshore wind farms, situated in coastal areas, provide even greater potential for harnessing wind energy due to strong and consistent winds. Moreover, the development of energy storage systems allows for the efficient utilization of wind energy during periods of low wind speeds or high electricity demand.

While wind energy has numerous advantages, it also faces challenges. The intermittency of wind and the need for backup power sources during periods of low wind speeds remain an issue. However, with the integration of smart grids and energy storage technologies, these challenges can be overcome.

In conclusion, wind energy is a vital component of sustainable energy systems and holds great promise for addressing the global energy crisis. Its renewable nature, environmental benefits, and economic potential make it an attractive option for environmental engineering professionals and anyone interested in transitioning to a more sustainable future. By embracing wind energy, we can power the future while protecting the environment for generations to come.

Hydropower

Hydropower: Harnessing the Power of Water for a Sustainable Future

Introduction:

In our quest for sustainable energy, hydropower emerges as a frontrunner in the race to combat climate change and reduce our dependence on fossil fuels. This subchapter explores the fascinating world of hydropower, its various forms, and its immense potential to shape a cleaner and greener future for all.

Harnessing the Power of Water:

Hydropower, also known as hydroelectric power, is the conversion of the energy of flowing or falling water into electricity. It has been used for centuries, dating back to ancient civilizations who used waterwheels to grind grain or saw wood. Today, modern hydropower systems utilize turbines and generators to produce clean, renewable electricity on a large scale.

Forms of Hydropower:

There are two main types of hydropower systems: reservoir-based and run-of-river. Reservoir-based systems involve the construction of large dams and reservoirs to store water, which is then released under controlled conditions to drive turbines. Run-of-river systems, on the other hand, do not require dams and instead use the natural flow of rivers to generate electricity. Both systems have their advantages and considerations, and their selection depends on factors such as geography, environment, and available resources.

Environmental Benefits:

Hydropower offers numerous environmental benefits, making it a crucial tool in the fight against climate change. Firstly, it is a renewable energy source, meaning it relies on the continuous water cycle rather than finite fossil fuel reserves. Secondly, hydropower produces no direct greenhouse gas emissions, helping to reduce our carbon footprint. Additionally, reservoir-based systems can provide flood control and water storage for irrigation, enhancing water management and supporting agricultural practices.

Challenges and Solutions:

While hydropower presents significant advantages, it is not without challenges. The construction of large dams can disrupt ecosystems, alter river flows, and displace communities. However, technological advancements and improved design practices have led to the emergence of low-impact hydropower projects, which aim to minimize environmental and social impacts. These projects prioritize ecosystem preservation, fish passage solutions, and community engagement to ensure sustainable development.

Conclusion:

Hydropower represents a key pillar of sustainable energy systems for everyone. Its ability to generate clean electricity, provide water management solutions, and contribute to climate change mitigation makes it an invaluable resource. By embracing the potential of hydropower and adopting responsible practices, we can harness the power of water to create a more sustainable future for ourselves and generations to come.

Geothermal Energy

Geothermal energy, a form of renewable energy, harnesses the heat from Earth's core to generate electricity and provide heating and cooling for various applications. This incredible source of power has been utilized for centuries, but it is only in recent years that its true potential has been realized. In this subchapter, we will explore the fascinating world of geothermal energy and its significance in powering our sustainable future.

Geothermal energy is derived from the natural heat stored within the Earth. The Earth's core, which reaches temperatures exceeding 5,000 degrees Celsius (9,000 degrees Fahrenheit), transfers heat to the surrounding rocks and water. This heat can be accessed through geothermal power plants, where steam or hot water is extracted from underground reservoirs. The steam is then used to drive turbines, generating electricity in a sustainable and emission-free manner.

One of the key advantages of geothermal energy is its consistency and reliability. Unlike solar or wind power, which depend on weather conditions, geothermal energy is available 24/7, making it an ideal baseload power source. Additionally, geothermal power plants have a small physical footprint and produce minimal greenhouse gas emissions, making them environmentally friendly alternatives to traditional fossil fuel power plants.

Geothermal energy can also be utilized for heating and cooling purposes. Geothermal heat pumps efficiently transfer heat from the ground to buildings for heating during colder months. In summer, the process is reversed, cooling buildings by transferring heat back into the ground. This technology significantly reduces energy consumption and lowers greenhouse gas emissions associated with traditional heating and cooling systems.

Environmental engineers play a crucial role in maximizing the potential of geothermal energy. They design and implement geothermal power plants, ensuring effective utilization of this sustainable energy source. They also conduct feasibility studies, assessing the viability of geothermal projects based on geological conditions and environmental impacts.

By embracing geothermal energy, we can reduce our dependence on fossil fuels and mitigate the adverse effects of climate change. As environmental engineering professionals, it is our responsibility to contribute to the development and utilization of sustainable energy systems. Geothermal energy represents a promising avenue for achieving a greener and more sustainable future for everyone.

In the next subchapter, we will delve into another fascinating form of renewable energy: tidal and wave power. Stay tuned to continue our journey through the diverse world of sustainable energy systems.

Biomass Energy

In today's world, where concerns about climate change and sustainable energy sources are at the forefront, biomass energy has emerged as a promising solution. Biomass refers to any organic matter derived from plants or animals that can be converted into usable energy. This subchapter will explore the potential of biomass energy and its role in powering a sustainable future.

Biomass energy has been used by humans for centuries, from burning wood for heat to using animal waste as fertilizer. However, recent advancements in technology have allowed us to harness biomass energy more efficiently and on a larger scale. By utilizing various conversion methods such as combustion, gasification, and fermentation, biomass can be transformed into heat, electricity, and even biofuels.

One of the key advantages of biomass energy is its renewable nature. Unlike fossil fuels, which are finite resources, biomass can be continuously grown and replenished. This makes biomass energy a sustainable alternative that helps reduce our dependence on fossil fuels, mitigating the environmental impact associated with their extraction and combustion.

Furthermore, biomass energy has the potential to significantly reduce greenhouse gas emissions. When biomass is burned or converted into biofuels, it releases carbon dioxide (CO_2) into the atmosphere. However, this CO_2 is part of a natural carbon cycle, where the plants used for biomass growth absorb an equivalent amount of CO_2 during photosynthesis. This balance makes biomass energy carbon-neutral, meaning it does not contribute to the net increase of CO_2 in the atmosphere.

In addition to its environmental benefits, biomass energy also presents economic opportunities. The cultivation and processing of biomass crops can create jobs and stimulate rural economies. Moreover, biomass energy can help diversify energy sources, reducing reliance on imported fuels and enhancing energy security.

However, like any energy source, biomass has its limitations and challenges. Ensuring sustainable biomass production is crucial to avoid negative impacts on land use, water resources, and biodiversity. Careful management and monitoring are necessary to avoid deforestation or the conversion of valuable agricultural land into energy crops.

In conclusion, biomass energy holds great promise as a renewable and sustainable energy source. Its ability to reduce greenhouse gas emissions and provide economic opportunities make it a viable option for powering our future. However, responsible and sustainable practices are essential to maximize its benefits while minimizing potential drawbacks. By embracing biomass energy as part of a diverse energy portfolio, we can move closer to a cleaner and more sustainable future for everyone.

Chapter 3: Harnessing Solar Energy

Photovoltaic Systems

In recent years, sustainable energy has become an increasingly important topic for individuals and industries alike. One of the most promising and widely used sources of renewable energy is photovoltaic (PV) systems. This subchapter aims to provide a comprehensive overview of PV systems, their components, and their significance in the realm of sustainable energy.

Photovoltaic systems are designed to convert sunlight directly into electricity through the use of solar panels. These panels consist of multiple interconnected solar cells made from semiconductor materials, typically silicon. When sunlight strikes these cells, it excites electrons, creating an electric current. This current can then be harnessed and used to power various electrical devices.

The installation of PV systems offers numerous benefits, both for individuals and the environment. Firstly, PV systems provide a clean and renewable source of energy, reducing dependence on fossil fuels and mitigating the harmful effects of greenhouse gas emissions. Additionally, PV systems can be installed on various scales, from small residential setups to large-scale solar farms, making them adaptable to different needs and locations.

For homeowners, PV systems offer the opportunity to generate their own electricity, reducing reliance on the grid and potentially lowering energy bills. Furthermore, excess energy produced by PV systems can be fed back into the grid, allowing homeowners to earn credits or sell electricity to utility companies. This creates a more decentralized and resilient energy system.

In the field of environmental engineering, PV systems play a crucial role in sustainable development. Their widespread adoption can help countries achieve their renewable energy targets and reduce their carbon footprint. Moreover, PV systems can be integrated into building designs, such as solar roofs and facades, blending functionality with aesthetics.

However, despite their numerous advantages, PV systems face certain challenges. The intermittent nature of sunlight requires the development of effective energy storage solutions, such as batteries, to ensure a continuous and reliable power supply. Additionally, the cost of PV systems, although decreasing, can still be a barrier for some individuals and communities.

Overall, photovoltaic systems hold enormous potential in the transition towards a sustainable energy future. By harnessing the power of the sun, we can reduce our reliance on fossil fuels, combat climate change, and create a more resilient and decentralized energy system. Whether you are an individual homeowner or an environmental engineering professional, understanding and embracing photovoltaic systems is crucial for a sustainable future.

Solar Thermal Systems

Solar thermal systems are a vital component of sustainable energy systems, harnessing the power of the sun to provide clean and renewable energy. These systems utilize the sun's heat to generate electricity, heat water, or provide space heating and cooling. In this subchapter, we will explore the various types of solar thermal systems, their applications, and their benefits in the context of sustainable energy systems.

One of the most common types of solar thermal systems is the solar water heater. This system captures the sun's energy and uses it to heat water for domestic or commercial use. Solar water heaters consist of solar collectors, which absorb sunlight and convert it into heat, and a storage tank to store the heated water. These systems are not only cost-effective in the long run but also reduce the reliance on fossil fuels, thereby decreasing greenhouse gas emissions.

Another type of solar thermal system is the solar air heater, which utilizes the sun's energy to heat air for space heating or drying applications. These systems consist of a solar collector that absorbs sunlight and transfers the heat to the air passing through it. Solar air heaters are particularly useful in colder climates, where space heating is essential. By utilizing solar thermal systems for space heating, we can significantly reduce our dependence on fossil fuels for heating purposes, leading to a substantial decrease in carbon emissions.

Solar thermal power plants are another significant application of solar thermal systems. These power plants use large arrays of mirrors or lenses to focus sunlight onto a receiver, which then heats a fluid to generate steam. The steam drives a turbine, which produces electricity. Solar thermal power plants are a clean and renewable alternative to conventional fossil fuel-based power plants, as they do not produce any greenhouse gas emissions during operation.

In conclusion, solar thermal systems offer a multitude of benefits in the context of sustainable energy systems. They provide clean and renewable energy for heating, cooling, and electricity generation, reducing our reliance on fossil fuels and mitigating climate change. Whether you are an environmental engineer, a homeowner, or simply someone interested in sustainable energy, understanding solar thermal systems is essential for building a more sustainable future for everyone.

Concentrated Solar Power (CSP)

Concentrated Solar Power (CSP) is a groundbreaking technology that harnesses the energy from the sun to generate electricity. It is a sustainable and clean energy solution that holds great potential for addressing the global energy crisis and mitigating the adverse effects of climate change. This subchapter aims to provide a comprehensive understanding of CSP, its working principles, and its significance in the field of environmental engineering.

CSP utilizes mirrors or lenses to concentrate sunlight onto a small area, typically a receiver, which then converts the solar energy into heat. This heat is used to generate steam, which drives a turbine connected to a generator, producing electricity. Unlike photovoltaic panels that directly convert sunlight into electricity, CSP systems can store thermal energy for later use, allowing for continuous power generation even during cloudy periods or at night.

One of the key advantages of CSP is its ability to produce large-scale electricity. CSP plants can be built in arid regions with abundant sunlight, such as deserts, where they occupy vast areas of land. These power plants have the potential to generate electricity for entire cities or even countries, significantly reducing reliance on fossil fuel-based power sources. Moreover, CSP plants can be integrated with existing power grids, providing a reliable and sustainable energy source.

Another advantage of CSP is its potential for thermal energy storage. By incorporating molten salt or other innovative storage mediums, CSP can store excess thermal energy during periods of low demand and release it when needed. This feature enables CSP plants to continue generating electricity even after sunset, making them a highly reliable and dispatchable energy source.

From an environmental engineering perspective, CSP offers numerous benefits. By harnessing the power of the sun, CSP plants produce zero greenhouse gas emissions during operation, helping to combat climate change. Additionally, CSP plants can contribute to water conservation by utilizing dry cooling systems, which reduce water consumption compared to traditional power plants that rely on water for cooling purposes.

In conclusion, Concentrated Solar Power (CSP) is a promising technology that has the potential to revolutionize the global energy landscape. Its ability to generate large-scale, reliable, and emission-free electricity makes it a crucial tool in the fight against climate change. As environmental engineering professionals, it is essential to explore and promote the deployment of CSP systems, as they offer sustainable and clean energy solutions for everyone. With continuous advancements and increased investments, CSP has the potential to power the future and create a more sustainable world for generations to come.

Solar Energy Storage and Grid Integration

As the world increasingly turns towards renewable energy sources, solar power has emerged as a leading contender in the quest for sustainable energy systems. Harnessing the power of the sun, solar energy offers a clean and abundant source of electricity. However, one of the challenges of solar power lies in its intermittent nature, as the sun does not shine 24/7. To address this issue, solar energy storage and grid integration have become crucial components of the sustainable energy ecosystem.

Solar energy storage refers to the process of capturing and storing excess solar energy generated during peak production periods for later use when the sun is not shining. This allows for a more reliable and consistent supply of electricity, even during periods of low solar irradiance. Various technologies are being developed for solar energy storage, including batteries, thermal storage systems, and pumped hydro storage. These storage solutions enable the deployment of solar power on a larger scale and help offset the intermittency of solar energy generation.

Grid integration plays a vital role in maximizing the benefits of solar power. By connecting solar energy systems to the electrical grid, excess energy can be fed back into the grid during times of high production, and electricity can be drawn from the grid when solar production is low. This two-way flow of electricity ensures a stable power supply and allows solar energy to be shared among different users. Grid integration also facilitates the integration of other renewable energy sources, such as wind and hydro, creating a diverse and resilient energy mix.

For environmental engineering professionals, understanding solar energy storage and grid integration is essential for developing sustainable energy systems. By incorporating these concepts into their designs and projects, they can contribute to reducing greenhouse gas emissions and mitigating the impacts of climate change. Environmental engineers play a vital role in optimizing the efficiency and effectiveness of solar energy storage technologies, ensuring that they are environmentally friendly and economically viable.

For the wider audience, solar energy storage and grid integration offer numerous benefits. By utilizing solar power and storing excess energy, individuals and communities can reduce their reliance on fossil fuels, lower their electricity bills, and contribute to a cleaner and healthier environment. Solar energy storage systems also provide backup power during grid outages, enhancing energy security and resilience.

In conclusion, solar energy storage and grid integration are pivotal aspects of sustainable energy systems. By addressing the intermittent nature of solar power and enabling the seamless integration of renewable energy sources, these technologies pave the way for a future powered by clean and reliable energy. Whether you are an environmental engineering professional or an individual interested in sustainable energy, understanding solar energy storage and grid integration is essential for embracing a greener future.

Chapter 4: Utilizing Wind Power

Wind Turbines and Wind Farms

In recent years, there has been a growing interest in harnessing the power of wind as a sustainable energy source. Wind turbines and wind farms have emerged as key players in the renewable energy sector, providing a clean and efficient alternative to traditional fossil fuel-based power generation. In this subchapter, we will explore the fascinating world of wind turbines and wind farms, and their significance in shaping a sustainable future.

Wind turbines are devices specifically designed to convert the kinetic energy of the wind into electricity. These towering structures consist of three main components: the rotor, the generator, and the tower. The rotor, which is typically composed of two or three blades, captures the energy from the wind as it flows through. As the blades rotate, the kinetic energy is transferred to the generator, where it is converted into electrical energy. The tower provides stability and height, enabling the turbine to capture stronger and more consistent winds at higher altitudes.

Wind farms, on the other hand, are collections of wind turbines strategically located in areas with high wind potential. By clustering multiple turbines together, wind farms can generate a significant amount of electricity, making them a viable alternative to conventional power plants. These sprawling installations are carefully planned to maximize energy production while minimizing environmental impact. Environmental engineers play a crucial role in this process, conducting thorough assessments to ensure that wind farms are designed and implemented in a manner that minimizes harm to local ecosystems and wildlife.

One of the greatest advantages of wind turbines and wind farms is their ability to generate clean and renewable energy. Unlike fossil fuels, wind power does not produce harmful greenhouse gas emissions or contribute to climate change. Additionally, wind energy is abundant, widely available, and inexhaustible, making it a reliable source of power for years to come.

Moreover, wind turbines have a relatively small physical footprint compared to other forms of power generation. This allows for the utilization of large areas of land for agricultural or other purposes while still harnessing the power of the wind. Furthermore, the economic benefits of wind farms cannot be overlooked. These projects create jobs, stimulate local economies, and reduce dependence on imported fossil fuels, thereby enhancing energy security and promoting sustainable development.

In conclusion, wind turbines and wind farms have emerged as significant contributors to sustainable energy systems. Combining technological innovation with environmental engineering expertise, these structures are helping to revolutionize the way we generate electricity. By harnessing the power of the wind, we can reduce our reliance on fossil fuels, mitigate climate change, and secure a cleaner, greener future for everyone.

Offshore Wind Energy

In recent years, the pursuit of sustainable energy sources has gained significant momentum. As the world continues to grapple with the challenges of climate change and dwindling fossil fuel reserves, alternative sources of energy are being explored. One such source that holds immense potential is offshore wind energy.

Offshore wind energy refers to the harnessing of wind power from turbines installed in bodies of water, usually in the ocean. This method offers several advantages over onshore wind farms, making it an increasingly popular choice for sustainable energy production.

Firstly, offshore wind farms tend to experience stronger, more consistent winds compared to onshore locations. This is due to the absence of obstructions such as buildings and hills, allowing for a more efficient conversion of wind energy into electricity. Additionally, offshore wind farms can be situated closer to densely populated areas, reducing transmission losses and making it easier to connect to the existing power grid.

Furthermore, offshore wind farms have a smaller environmental impact compared to other forms of energy generation. They do not require large areas of land, thereby minimizing the disruption of natural habitats. Additionally, offshore wind farms have the potential to play a crucial role in mitigating climate change by reducing greenhouse gas emissions. By replacing traditional fossil fuel-based power plants, offshore wind energy significantly reduces carbon dioxide emissions and helps combat global warming.

However, the development of offshore wind farms does come with its own set of challenges. The construction and maintenance of offshore wind turbines require specialized equipment and expertise, making it a costly venture. Moreover, the harsh marine environment poses additional technical and logistical challenges. However, advancements in technology and engineering solutions have helped overcome many of these obstacles, making offshore wind energy a viable and sustainable option.

In conclusion, offshore wind energy represents a promising avenue for sustainable energy production. Its ability to harness strong and consistent winds, coupled with its minimal environmental impact, make it an attractive choice for addressing the world's energy needs. While challenges exist, ongoing research and development in the field of offshore wind energy promise to make it an increasingly viable and cost-effective solution. By embracing offshore wind energy, we can take a significant step towards a cleaner and more sustainable future for everyone.

Wind Energy Storage and Grid Integration

In recent years, wind energy has emerged as a promising source of renewable power. Its ability to harness the natural force of the wind and convert it into clean electricity has captivated the attention of environmental engineers and energy enthusiasts alike. However, the intermittent nature of wind can pose challenges in its integration into the existing power grid. This subchapter explores the concept of wind energy storage and its grid integration, offering insights into the key technologies and strategies employed to maximize the potential of wind energy.

Wind energy storage plays a crucial role in ensuring a stable and reliable supply of electricity. As wind turbines generate power only when the wind blows, excess electricity needs to be stored for times when the wind is not blowing. Various storage technologies have been developed to address this issue. One such technology is battery storage, which involves storing excess wind energy in batteries and using it during periods of low wind activity. Other storage methods, such as flywheels and compressed air energy storage, offer alternative solutions for capturing and releasing wind energy as needed.

Integrating wind energy into the power grid requires careful planning and coordination. Environmental engineers play a vital role in designing and implementing effective grid integration strategies. Grid operators need to balance the fluctuating supply of wind energy with the demand for electricity, ensuring a stable and reliable power supply. This involves employing advanced forecasting techniques to predict wind patterns and adjusting the operation of conventional power plants accordingly.

Moreover, grid integration of wind energy necessitates the development of smart grids. These intelligent systems enable real-time communication between power generators, consumers, and grid operators, allowing for efficient management of electricity flow. By integrating wind energy with other renewable sources, such as solar and hydroelectric power, a diverse and resilient energy mix can be achieved. This not only enhances the reliability of the grid but also reduces dependence on fossil fuels, contributing to a cleaner and more sustainable future.

In conclusion, wind energy storage and grid integration are crucial components of a sustainable energy system. Environmental engineers play a vital role in designing and implementing effective storage technologies and grid integration strategies. By leveraging advancements in technology and embracing the potential of smart grids, wind energy can be harnessed to its fullest extent, providing a clean and reliable source of power for everyone. As we continue to strive towards a greener future, wind energy storage and grid integration will undoubtedly play a pivotal role in powering the world sustainably.

Chapter 5: Tapping into Hydropower Resources

Run-of-River Hydropower

Run-of-river hydropower is a sustainable energy system that harnesses the power of flowing water to generate electricity. Unlike traditional hydropower plants that require large reservoirs and dams to store water, run-of-river systems are designed to operate with minimal water storage and rely on the natural flow of rivers and streams.

One of the primary advantages of run-of-river hydropower is its low environmental impact. By harnessing the kinetic energy of flowing water, this system produces clean and renewable electricity without requiring the construction of large dams. This means that there is no significant disruption to the natural flow of rivers and no displacement of local communities or wildlife habitats. Run-of-river hydropower also eliminates the need for massive reservoirs, which can lead to the submergence of vast areas of land, loss of biodiversity, and the release of methane from decaying organic matter.

Another benefit of run-of-river hydropower is its reliability and predictability. Unlike solar or wind energy, which can be intermittent and dependent on weather conditions, rivers and streams typically maintain a consistent flow throughout the year. This makes run-of-river systems a reliable source of electricity, especially in regions with stable and predictable water resources.

In terms of operation, run-of-river hydropower plants consist of diversion structures that redirect a portion of the flowing water into a channel or penstock. The water is then channeled through a turbine, where its kinetic energy is converted into mechanical energy. The mechanical energy is further transformed into electrical energy by a generator connected to the turbine. After passing through the turbine, the water is returned to the river downstream without significant alteration.

Run-of-river hydropower is an ideal solution for environmental engineers and anyone interested in sustainable energy systems. It offers a viable alternative to fossil fuel-based electricity generation, reducing greenhouse gas emissions and mitigating climate change. Moreover, it provides an opportunity for local communities to generate their own clean energy, fostering energy independence and economic development.

As we strive towards a more sustainable future, run-of-river hydropower represents a promising avenue for meeting our energy needs while preserving the environment. By harnessing the power of flowing water, we can create a greener and more resilient energy system for everyone.

Reservoir Hydropower

Reservoir hydropower, also known as conventional hydropower, is a well-established and reliable source of renewable energy. It involves the use of dams and reservoirs to store water, which is then released in a controlled manner to drive turbines and generate electricity. This subchapter explores the various aspects and benefits of reservoir hydropower, shedding light on its relevance in sustainable energy systems for everyone.

One of the primary advantages of reservoir hydropower is its ability to provide a consistent and reliable source of electricity. Unlike other renewable energy sources like solar or wind, which are intermittent, reservoir hydropower can operate continuously, providing a steady supply of power. This stability is particularly crucial for industries and communities that require a constant and uninterrupted energy supply.

Furthermore, reservoir hydropower offers a unique opportunity for energy storage. By storing water in the reservoir during periods of low electricity demand, excess power can be generated during peak periods or when renewable sources like solar and wind are not available. This storage capacity enhances the overall efficiency of the energy system and helps balance the grid, ensuring a stable and reliable power supply.

Another significant advantage of reservoir hydropower is its ability to provide multiple benefits beyond electricity generation. These include flood control, irrigation, and water supply for domestic and industrial use. Dams built for hydropower purposes can regulate river flows, mitigating the risk of flooding downstream. Additionally, the water stored in reservoirs can be used for irrigation, facilitating agricultural practices and boosting food production. This multi-purpose nature of reservoir hydropower makes it an attractive option for environmental engineering projects aimed at sustainable water management.

However, it is essential to consider the environmental impacts associated with reservoir hydropower. The construction of dams can result in the displacement of local communities and the loss of natural habitats. Additionally, the alteration of river flows and water quality can have significant ecological consequences. Therefore, it is crucial to implement appropriate measures to mitigate these impacts, such as fish ladders to facilitate fish migration and water release strategies that mimic natural flow patterns.

In conclusion, reservoir hydropower plays a vital role in sustainable energy systems and environmental engineering projects. Its ability to provide consistent and reliable power, as well as its capacity for energy storage and multiple benefits beyond electricity generation, make it an attractive option for a wide range of applications. However, careful planning and implementation are necessary to minimize the environmental impacts associated with dams and reservoirs, ensuring a balanced and sustainable approach to harnessing this valuable renewable energy resource.

Pumped Storage Hydropower

Pumped Storage Hydropower: Harnessing the Power of Water for Sustainable Energy

Introduction:

In our quest for sustainable energy systems, it is crucial to explore innovative solutions that can meet our growing energy demands while minimizing environmental impacts. One such solution is Pumped Storage Hydropower (PSH), a remarkable technology that utilizes the power of water to store and generate electricity. In this subchapter, we will delve into the intricacies of PSH, highlighting its benefits, challenges, and potential for widespread implementation.

Understanding Pumped Storage Hydropower:

Pumped Storage Hydropower is an advanced method of energy storage that combines two reservoirs at different elevations with a reversible turbine system. During periods of excess electricity supply, such as low-demand hours or when renewable sources produce surplus energy, the excess electricity is used to pump water from a lower reservoir to an upper reservoir. Then, during peak demand periods or when renewable energy sources are unable to meet electricity demand, the stored water is released through the turbines to generate electricity.

Benefits of Pumped Storage Hydropower:

1. Grid Stability: PSH provides crucial grid stabilization by balancing supply and demand fluctuations. It can quickly respond to changes in electricity demand, ensuring a reliable and stable power supply.

2. Energy Storage: PSH allows for efficient energy storage on a large scale. It enables excess energy to be stored during low-demand periods and then released when demand is high, reducing the need for fossil fuel-based electricity generation during peak hours.

3. Renewable Integration: PSH complements intermittent renewable energy sources like wind and solar by providing a reliable backup energy source. It helps bridge the gap between energy generation and demand, ensuring continuous electricity supply.

Challenges and Future Prospects:

While PSH offers numerous benefits, it faces some challenges as well. Constructing large-scale reservoirs can have significant environmental impacts, including land displacement and alteration of aquatic habitats. However, advancements in technology are addressing these concerns by exploring alternatives, such as underground reservoirs or utilizing existing water bodies.

In the future, PSH has tremendous potential to play a vital role in sustainable energy systems. As the world transitions towards a greener energy mix, PSH can contribute to reducing greenhouse gas emissions, enhancing grid flexibility, and improving overall energy efficiency.

Conclusion:

Pumped Storage Hydropower represents a promising solution for a sustainable energy future. By harnessing the power of water, PSH offers a reliable and efficient method of energy storage, helping balance electricity supply and demand, integrating renewable energy sources, and ensuring grid stability. While challenges exist, ongoing advancements in technology and greater environmental consciousness will pave the way for the widespread adoption of PSH. Embracing this technology will not only contribute to a more sustainable energy system but also create a cleaner and greener future for generations to come.

Small-Scale Hydropower

Hydropower has long been recognized as one of the most reliable and sustainable sources of renewable energy. While large-scale hydropower plants have dominated the industry for decades, there is a growing interest in small-scale hydropower systems. In this subchapter, we will explore the concept of small-scale hydropower and its potential as a sustainable energy solution.

Small-scale hydropower refers to the generation of electricity from water flow on a relatively small scale, typically from rivers, streams, or even irrigation canals. Unlike large-scale hydropower projects that require massive dams and reservoirs, small-scale systems can be installed in smaller water bodies, making them more accessible and environmentally friendly.

One of the key advantages of small-scale hydropower is its potential to provide electricity to remote communities or areas with limited access to the power grid. These systems can be installed in rural areas, harnessing the power of nearby rivers or streams to generate electricity for local use. This can greatly improve the quality of life for people living in these areas, allowing them to access modern amenities and improve their economic opportunities.

Another benefit of small-scale hydropower is its minimal impact on the environment. Unlike large dams that can disrupt ecosystems and cause displacement of communities, small-scale systems have a much smaller footprint. They can be designed to minimize environmental impact by incorporating fish-friendly turbines and maintaining the natural flow of water.

Small-scale hydropower can also be a cost-effective solution for individuals or communities looking to reduce their reliance on fossil fuels. Once installed, these systems have low operational costs and can provide a consistent and reliable source of electricity. Additionally, some small-scale hydropower projects may be eligible for government incentives or subsidies, further reducing the financial burden of implementation.

However, it is important to note that small-scale hydropower is not suitable for every location. The feasibility of a project depends on factors such as water flow, land availability, and environmental considerations. A thorough assessment and feasibility study must be conducted before implementing a small-scale hydropower system.

In conclusion, small-scale hydropower holds great potential as a sustainable energy solution, particularly in remote areas with limited access to the power grid. Its minimal environmental impact, cost-effectiveness, and reliability make it an attractive option for individuals, communities, and even small industries. As we strive towards a more sustainable future, small-scale hydropower can play an important role in diversifying our energy sources and reducing our carbon footprint.

Chapter 6: Exploring Geothermal Energy

Geothermal Power Plants

Geothermal power plants are a fascinating and sustainable source of energy that harnesses the Earth's natural heat to generate electricity. In this subchapter, we will explore the inner workings of geothermal power plants, their benefits, and how they contribute to a more sustainable future.

Geothermal power plants tap into the heat stored beneath the Earth's surface. This heat originates from the Earth's core and is continuously produced by the decay of radioactive elements. The geothermal energy is then harnessed using various techniques, such as drilling deep wells into hot rocks or capturing hot water and steam from underground reservoirs.

One of the main advantages of geothermal power plants is their reliability. Unlike solar or wind power, geothermal energy is available 24/7, regardless of weather conditions. This makes it a stable and consistent source of electricity, providing a reliable base load for our energy needs.

Moreover, geothermal power plants have a minimal environmental impact compared to fossil fuel-based power plants. They produce almost no greenhouse gas emissions and have a small land footprint. Unlike other renewable energy sources, geothermal power plants do not rely on external factors such as wind or sunlight, making them highly efficient and independent energy systems.

Geothermal power plants also offer additional benefits beyond electricity generation. The hot water and steam extracted during the process can be used for heating purposes, such as district heating systems or industrial processes. This co-generation of heat and power makes geothermal energy even more economically viable and appealing.

In recent years, advancements in geothermal technology have made it more accessible and cost-effective. Innovations in drilling techniques and equipment have reduced the upfront costs associated with geothermal power plant construction. As a result, more countries around the world are investing in geothermal energy, harnessing this abundant and clean source of power.

For environmental engineering professionals, geothermal power plants present exciting opportunities. By understanding the geology, engineering techniques, and environmental considerations involved, they can contribute to the development and design of sustainable geothermal projects. Their expertise can help optimize the efficiency of geothermal power plants and ensure their seamless integration into existing energy systems.

In conclusion, geothermal power plants are a promising and sustainable solution to our energy needs. With their reliability, minimal environmental impact, and potential for co-generation, they offer a practical and efficient way to power our future. Environmental engineering professionals have a crucial role to play in advancing geothermal technology and driving the transition towards a more sustainable energy system for everyone.

Direct Use of Geothermal Energy

Geothermal energy, derived from the Earth's heat, has emerged as a promising alternative to traditional energy sources. While most people associate geothermal energy with electricity generation, there is another valuable application: direct use. This subchapter explores the direct use of geothermal energy and its potential to revolutionize sustainable energy systems.

Direct use of geothermal energy involves utilizing the Earth's heat directly for various purposes, such as heating buildings, drying crops, or even providing hot water for domestic use. It offers a multitude of benefits, making it an attractive option for both individuals and communities.

One of the primary advantages of direct geothermal energy use is its environmental friendliness. Unlike fossil fuels, which contribute to greenhouse gas emissions and air pollution, geothermal energy is clean and renewable. By harnessing the Earth's heat, we can significantly reduce our carbon footprint and mitigate climate change. This makes it an ideal choice for environmental engineers seeking sustainable energy solutions.

Moreover, direct geothermal energy use is highly efficient. Traditional heating systems often waste energy during the conversion process. However, geothermal energy directly taps into the Earth's heat, eliminating the need for energy conversion. This improves overall efficiency and reduces energy costs, making it an economically viable option for individuals and communities.

Direct geothermal energy use also offers energy independence. By utilizing the Earth's heat, communities can become self-sufficient in meeting their energy needs. This reduces reliance on external energy sources and enhances energy security. In regions where access to traditional energy sources is limited, direct geothermal energy use can have a transformative impact on people's lives.

Furthermore, direct geothermal energy use promotes local economic development. By investing in geothermal infrastructure, communities can create jobs and stimulate economic growth. Geothermal power plants, district heating systems, and other related industries require skilled workers, fostering employment opportunities in the field of environmental engineering.

As we strive towards a sustainable future, it is crucial to explore all available options. The direct use of geothermal energy presents a viable and practical solution to our energy needs. Its environmental benefits, high efficiency, energy independence, and economic potential make it an attractive choice for individuals and communities alike.

In conclusion, direct geothermal energy use offers a sustainable alternative to traditional energy sources. Its advantages in terms of environmental friendliness, efficiency, energy independence, and economic development make it a compelling option for environmental engineers and individuals seeking sustainable energy solutions. By harnessing the Earth's heat, we can power a greener and more prosperous future for everyone.

Geothermal Heat Pumps

Geothermal heat pumps are an innovative and sustainable solution for heating and cooling buildings. This advanced technology harnesses the Earth's natural heat to provide energy-efficient and eco-friendly heating and cooling systems for homes, offices, and other structures. In this subchapter, we will explore the concept, benefits, and practical applications of geothermal heat pumps, offering a comprehensive understanding of this promising technology.

Geothermal heat pumps work by utilizing the constant temperature below the Earth's surface. This temperature remains relatively stable throughout the year, regardless of the weather or climate conditions above ground. The heat pump system consists of a network of pipes, called a ground loop, buried underground. This loop circulates a fluid, usually a mixture of water and antifreeze, which absorbs the geothermal heat from the ground. The heat is then transferred to a heat exchanger within the heat pump system, where it can be used to heat or cool a building.

One of the main advantages of geothermal heat pumps is their high energy efficiency. Unlike traditional heating and cooling systems that rely on burning fossil fuels or consuming electricity, geothermal heat pumps can achieve up to 400% efficiency. For every unit of electricity consumed to power the heat pump, four units of heat can be extracted from the Earth. This not only reduces greenhouse gas emissions but also lowers energy bills and dependence on non-renewable energy sources.

Furthermore, geothermal heat pumps have a long lifespan and require minimal maintenance compared to conventional systems. They are also exceptionally quiet during operation, enhancing the comfort of living and working environments. Additionally, geothermal energy is a reliable and consistent renewable energy source, making it an ideal choice for environmentally conscious individuals and businesses.

The applications of geothermal heat pumps are vast and varied. They can be used in residential buildings, commercial spaces, and even agricultural facilities. Whether it's heating or cooling, geothermal heat pumps can meet the needs of any structure while significantly reducing the carbon footprint. Moreover, governments and organizations around the world are increasingly recognizing the potential of geothermal energy and offering incentives and subsidies for its adoption.

In conclusion, geothermal heat pumps provide an effective and sustainable solution for heating and cooling systems. With their exceptional energy efficiency, longevity, and minimal environmental impact, they are a clear choice for a greener future. By harnessing the Earth's natural heat, we can power our buildings and mitigate climate change, making geothermal heat pumps a crucial technology for everyone concerned about sustainable energy systems.

Enhanced Geothermal Systems (EGS)

Geothermal energy has emerged as a promising and sustainable alternative to traditional energy sources. In recent years, the development of Enhanced Geothermal Systems (EGS) has opened up new possibilities for harnessing the Earth's natural heat and transforming it into a reliable and clean source of power. This subchapter introduces EGS and its potential to revolutionize the field of sustainable energy.

EGS is a technology that enables the extraction of geothermal energy from areas with low natural permeability. Unlike traditional geothermal systems, which require naturally occurring permeability to function efficiently, EGS creates artificial reservoirs to tap into the Earth's heat. This technology involves drilling deep into the Earth's crust and injecting water into hot rock formations. The water circulates through the fractures in the rock, absorbing heat and returning to the surface as steam, which drives turbines to generate electricity.

One of the key advantages of EGS is its versatility. Unlike other renewable energy sources that are dependent on specific geographical locations or weather conditions, geothermal energy can be harnessed almost anywhere on the planet. EGS technology allows us to unlock the potential of geothermal resources in areas where conventional geothermal systems are not viable, significantly expanding the scope of geothermal energy production.

EGS also has minimal environmental impact, making it an ideal choice for environmental engineering. Unlike fossil fuel-based power plants, geothermal power plants produce virtually no greenhouse gas emissions. Additionally, EGS does not rely on surface water resources, reducing the strain on local ecosystems. By tapping into the Earth's heat, we can reduce our reliance on fossil fuels and mitigate the effects of climate change.

Furthermore, EGS has the potential to provide a stable and consistent power supply. Unlike solar and wind energy, which are intermittent and dependent on weather conditions, geothermal energy is available 24/7. This baseload power capability makes it a reliable source of electricity, capable of meeting the demands of a growing population.

However, despite its immense potential, EGS is still in its early stages of development. The technology requires further research and investment to optimize its efficiency and reduce costs. Additionally, the process of creating artificial reservoirs can be challenging and may cause seismic activity if not properly managed. These issues highlight the need for ongoing research and strict regulatory frameworks to ensure the safe and sustainable implementation of EGS projects.

In conclusion, Enhanced Geothermal Systems offer a promising solution to our energy needs. With its versatility, minimal environmental impact, and reliable power supply, EGS has the potential to transform the energy landscape. As environmental engineers, it is crucial that we continue to explore and invest in this technology, unlocking the Earth's hidden heat and paving the way for a sustainable and greener future for everyone.

Chapter 7: Utilizing Biomass for Energy Production

Bioenergy Conversion Technologies

In the quest for sustainable energy systems, bioenergy conversion technologies have emerged as a promising solution. Harnessing the power of biomass, these technologies offer a renewable and environmentally friendly alternative to traditional fossil fuels. This subchapter explores the various bioenergy conversion technologies and their potential to power the future.

Bioenergy refers to the energy derived from organic matter, such as plants, crops, agricultural residues, and even animal waste. The conversion of biomass into usable energy can be achieved through several different processes, each with its unique advantages and challenges.

One of the most common bioenergy conversion technologies is the combustion of biomass. This involves burning organic matter to produce heat, which can then be used to generate electricity or provide heat for industrial processes. While combustion is relatively simple and widely practiced, it does release greenhouse gases and particulate matter into the atmosphere. To mitigate these emissions, advanced combustion technologies and emission control systems can be employed.

Another approach to bioenergy conversion is through the process of anaerobic digestion. This biological process involves the decomposition of organic matter in the absence of oxygen, resulting in the production of biogas. Biogas, consisting mainly of methane, can be utilized as a fuel for power generation or as a substitute for natural gas in heating applications. Anaerobic digestion not only produces renewable energy but also reduces the amount of organic waste going to landfills, thus contributing to waste management.

Pyrolysis and gasification are two other bioenergy conversion technologies that involve thermal decomposition of biomass. Pyrolysis converts biomass into bio-oil, which can be further processed into biofuels or used as a feedstock in the chemical industry. Gasification, on the other hand, converts biomass into a mixture of gases known as syngas, which can be utilized for power generation or as a raw material for the production of chemicals and fuels.

Bioenergy conversion technologies offer numerous benefits, including reduced greenhouse gas emissions, waste management solutions, and energy independence. However, their widespread adoption requires addressing challenges such as feedstock availability, technological advancements, and policy support.

As environmental engineering professionals, it is crucial to stay informed about bioenergy conversion technologies and their potential for sustainable energy systems. By understanding these technologies, we can contribute to the development of innovative solutions that address the environmental challenges we face today and power a sustainable future for everyone.

Biomass Power Plants

In the quest for sustainable energy systems, biomass power plants have emerged as a promising solution to the environmental challenges we face today. This subchapter will delve into the world of biomass power plants, exploring their benefits, working principles, and potential applications. Whether you are an environmental engineering enthusiast or simply someone interested in sustainable energy, this chapter will provide you with valuable insights into this fascinating field.

Biomass power plants harness the energy stored in organic materials such as wood, agricultural waste, and dedicated energy crops. Unlike fossil fuels, which release carbon dioxide into the atmosphere when burned, biomass materials are considered carbon-neutral since the carbon dioxide released during combustion is offset by the carbon absorbed during their growth. This makes biomass power plants an attractive option for reducing greenhouse gas emissions and combating climate change.

The working principle of biomass power plants involves the combustion of biomass materials to produce heat, which is then converted into electricity. The biomass feedstock is typically burned in a boiler to generate steam, which drives a turbine connected to a generator. This process is similar to conventional coal-fired power plants, but with a significantly lower carbon footprint and reduced environmental impact.

Beyond electricity generation, biomass power plants can also produce heat for industrial processes or district heating systems. Additionally, the residual ash from combustion can be used as a valuable fertilizer or construction material, further enhancing the sustainability of these plants.

The applications of biomass power plants are diverse and far-reaching. They can be integrated into existing energy infrastructure, replacing fossil fuel-based power plants and reducing dependence on finite resources. Furthermore, biomass power plants can be decentralized, allowing for local energy production and enhancing energy security.

However, it is important to consider the sustainability of biomass feedstocks. While utilizing agricultural waste and dedicated energy crops can minimize the impact on food production, careful planning and management are crucial to ensure the long-term viability of biomass power plants. Additionally, advancements in technology and research are continuously improving the efficiency of biomass conversion processes, making them more economically viable and environmentally friendly.

In conclusion, biomass power plants offer a sustainable and renewable alternative to conventional energy sources. They not only provide a means to generate electricity but also contribute to reducing greenhouse gas emissions and fostering a more sustainable future. By understanding the principles and potential of biomass power plants, we can collectively work towards a more environmentally friendly and resilient energy system for everyone.

Biogas and Anaerobic Digestion

In the quest for sustainable energy systems, biogas and anaerobic digestion have emerged as promising solutions that not only provide renewable energy but also address waste management challenges. This subchapter will delve into the fascinating world of biogas and anaerobic digestion, unlocking the potential they hold for a greener future.

Biogas, often referred to as renewable natural gas, is a versatile energy source derived from the breakdown of organic matter in the absence of oxygen. It can be produced from a wide range of organic materials, including agricultural waste, food waste, sewage sludge, and even dedicated energy crops. The process that harnesses biogas is called anaerobic digestion.

Anaerobic digestion involves a series of biochemical reactions that occur in the absence of oxygen, facilitated by a diverse microbial community. The process begins with the loading of organic material into a sealed digester, where it undergoes decomposition. During this process, organic matter is broken down by bacteria, producing a mixture of gases, mainly methane (CH_4) and carbon dioxide (CO_2). Methane, being the primary component of biogas, can be utilized as a renewable fuel for heating, electricity generation, or even as a vehicle fuel.

The advantages of biogas and anaerobic digestion are manifold. Firstly, they provide a renewable source of energy, reducing our dependence on fossil fuels and mitigating climate change impacts. Additionally, anaerobic digestion offers an environmentally friendly solution for organic waste management, reducing the release of greenhouse gases and odorous compounds associated with traditional waste disposal methods.

From an engineering standpoint, biogas and anaerobic digestion present exciting opportunities. Environmental engineers play a vital role in optimizing the process, from designing efficient digesters to controlling and monitoring the microbial communities involved. They also contribute to the development of advanced technologies that enhance biogas production efficiency and purity.

Moreover, the integration of biogas and anaerobic digestion into sustainable energy systems holds promise for decentralized energy production. Small-scale anaerobic digesters can be implemented on farms, in communities, or even individual households, enabling them to generate their own renewable energy and reduce energy costs.

In conclusion, biogas and anaerobic digestion are valuable tools in our journey towards sustainable energy systems. By harnessing the power of organic waste, they provide renewable energy, reduce greenhouse gas emissions, and contribute to waste management. Environmental engineers play a crucial role in optimizing and advancing these technologies, ensuring a greener future for everyone.

Biofuels for Transportation

In the quest for a sustainable future, the transportation sector plays a vital role. It is responsible for a significant portion of global greenhouse gas emissions, contributing to climate change and air pollution. However, there is a promising solution on the horizon - biofuels for transportation.

Biofuels are derived from renewable organic materials, such as crops, algae, or waste products, and can be used to power vehicles. They offer an alternative to fossil fuels, which are not only finite but also have detrimental environmental impacts. By transitioning to biofuels, we can significantly reduce our carbon footprint and create a cleaner and greener transportation sector.

One of the key advantages of biofuels is their potential to mitigate climate change. When burned, biofuels release carbon dioxide (CO_2), but the plants used to produce them absorb CO_2 from the atmosphere through photosynthesis. This creates a closed carbon cycle, where the CO_2 emitted during combustion is balanced by the CO_2 absorbed during growth. As a result, biofuels have a much lower net carbon emission compared to fossil fuels.

Moreover, biofuels offer a way to utilize agricultural waste and other organic materials that would otherwise go to landfill or emit greenhouse gases as they decompose. By converting these waste products into biofuels, we can reduce the release of harmful gases and prevent environmental pollution. This not only reduces our reliance on fossil fuels but also helps to address the issue of waste management.

In terms of environmental engineering, the development and implementation of biofuels for transportation require innovative technologies and infrastructure. Scientists and engineers are constantly researching and improving methods of biofuel production, optimizing efficiency, and reducing costs. Additionally, the transportation sector needs to adapt to accommodate the use of biofuels, such as developing compatible engines and fueling stations.

However, it is important to note that not all biofuels are created equal. Some biofuel production methods, such as large-scale monoculture farming, can have negative environmental and social implications, including deforestation and competition for land and water resources. Therefore, it is crucial to promote sustainable biofuel production practices that consider these factors and aim for a holistic approach to energy production.

In conclusion, biofuels for transportation hold great promise in our journey towards sustainable energy systems. They offer a renewable and cleaner alternative to fossil fuels, reducing carbon emissions and mitigating climate change. As environmental engineers, it is our responsibility to support and promote the development of sustainable biofuel technologies and ensure their implementation is conducted in an environmentally responsible manner. By embracing biofuels for transportation, we can pave the way for a more sustainable and greener future for everyone.

Chapter 8: Integrating Sustainable Energy Systems into Buildings

Energy-Efficient Design Principles

In today's world, where concerns about climate change and the depletion of natural resources are at the forefront, it has become imperative to adopt sustainable practices in every aspect of our lives. This includes the design and construction of our built environment. Energy-efficient design principles have emerged as a crucial aspect of environmental engineering, offering a path towards a more sustainable and greener future.

Energy-efficient design principles aim to minimize the energy consumption of buildings while maximizing their performance and comfort. By incorporating these principles into the design phase, architects and engineers can significantly reduce the environmental impact of new constructions and retrofit existing ones. The following are some key principles to consider:

Passive Design: One of the fundamental principles of energy-efficient design is to make the most of natural resources. Passive design utilizes the building's orientation, layout, and materials to optimize energy usage. By maximizing natural daylight, using shading techniques to reduce heat gain, and incorporating natural ventilation, buildings can minimize their reliance on artificial lighting, cooling, and heating systems.

Insulation and Air Sealing: Proper insulation and air sealing are critical to reducing energy waste. By ensuring that the building envelope is well-insulated and sealed, heat transfer and air infiltration can be minimized. This helps maintain a stable indoor temperature, reducing the need for excessive heating or cooling.

Energy-Efficient Lighting: Lighting accounts for a significant portion of a building's energy consumption. By using energy-efficient lighting fixtures such as LEDs and incorporating natural daylighting strategies, energy usage can be significantly reduced. Additionally, installing occupancy sensors and timers can further optimize energy consumption by automatically turning off lights when not in use.

Efficient HVAC Systems: Heating, ventilation, and air conditioning (HVAC) systems are major energy consumers in buildings. By using energy-efficient HVAC equipment, such as high-efficiency heat pumps or geothermal systems, and implementing smart controls that optimize energy usage based on occupancy and weather conditions, significant energy savings can be achieved.

Renewable Energy Integration: To further reduce dependence on fossil fuels, renewable energy sources such as solar panels or wind turbines can be integrated into the building's design. By generating clean energy on-site, buildings can reduce their carbon footprint and even become net-zero or net-positive energy structures.

By embracing energy-efficient design principles, we can create buildings that not only minimize their impact on the environment but also enhance user comfort and well-being. These principles are not limited to large-scale commercial projects but can be applied to residential buildings as well. From single-family homes to high-rise office towers, everyone can contribute to a sustainable future by incorporating energy-efficient design principles into their construction or renovation projects. Let us strive together to build a greener and more sustainable world for ourselves and the generations to come.

Passive Solar Design

Passive Solar Design: Harnessing the Sun's Energy for a Sustainable Future

Introduction:
In our quest for sustainable energy systems, we often overlook a readily available and abundant source of power: the sun. Passive solar design is a concept that ingeniously utilizes the sun's energy to heat, cool, and light our buildings, reducing our reliance on traditional energy sources. In this subchapter, we will explore the principles and benefits of passive solar design, providing a comprehensive guide for everyone interested in sustainable energy systems and specifically addressing the niche of environmental engineering.

Harnessing the Sun's Energy:
Passive solar design is centered around capturing, storing, and distributing solar energy without the use of mechanical or electrical devices. By strategically placing windows, using thermal mass materials, and optimizing building orientation, we can create spaces that naturally regulate their temperature and lighting.

Benefits of Passive Solar Design:
1. Energy Efficiency: Passive solar design can significantly reduce energy consumption by minimizing the need for artificial heating and cooling. This, in turn, reduces greenhouse gas emissions and lowers utility bills, making it economically and environmentally beneficial.

2. Enhanced Comfort: Buildings designed with passive solar principles provide greater thermal comfort, as they maintain more stable interior temperatures throughout the day. This reduces the need for

temperature adjustments, creating a comfortable living or working environment.

3. Improved Indoor Air Quality: Passive solar design promotes natural ventilation, allowing fresh air to circulate, reducing the buildup of pollutants, and enhancing the overall indoor air quality.

4. Cost Savings: By reducing the reliance on mechanical heating and cooling systems, passive solar design can lead to long-term cost savings in terms of maintenance and energy bills.

5. Adaptability: Passive solar design can be implemented in new construction projects or retrofitted into existing buildings, making it a versatile and adaptable solution for a sustainable future.

Considerations for Environmental Engineers: Environmental engineers play a crucial role in promoting and implementing passive solar design. They can utilize their expertise to analyze the local climate, site conditions, and building materials to optimize the design and maximize its benefits. Additionally, they can assess the potential environmental impacts, calculate energy savings, and ensure compliance with building codes and regulations.

Conclusion:
Passive solar design offers an innovative and sustainable approach to harnessing the sun's energy for building heating, cooling, and lighting. By adopting this design philosophy, we can create energy-efficient, comfortable, and environmentally friendly spaces. Environmental engineers, in particular, can lead the way in implementing passive solar design principles, contributing to a greener and more sustainable future for all.

Net-Zero Energy Buildings

In recent years, the concept of net-zero energy buildings has gained significant attention in the field of environmental engineering. These innovative structures are designed to produce as much energy as they consume, resulting in a net-zero energy balance. This subchapter explores the concept of net-zero energy buildings and their immense potential to revolutionize the way we think about sustainable energy systems.

Net-zero energy buildings are a beacon of hope for a greener future. By utilizing advanced technologies and design strategies, these buildings are able to generate renewable energy on-site, reducing their reliance on traditional power sources. Solar panels, wind turbines, and geothermal systems are just a few examples of the renewable energy sources commonly integrated into net-zero energy buildings. These structures not only minimize their environmental impact but also serve as an inspiration for a more sustainable way of life.

One of the key benefits of net-zero energy buildings is their potential to reduce greenhouse gas emissions. Traditional buildings are responsible for a significant portion of global carbon dioxide emissions, primarily due to their reliance on fossil fuel-based energy sources. By generating clean energy on-site, net-zero energy buildings drastically reduce their carbon footprint and contribute to mitigating climate change.

Additionally, net-zero energy buildings can significantly reduce energy costs for their occupants. With energy prices on the rise, the ability to generate one's own electricity becomes an incredibly attractive proposition. Not only do these buildings reduce monthly utility bills, but they also provide a sense of energy independence and resilience in the face of power outages or disruptions.

The adoption of net-zero energy buildings has been steadily increasing, with governments, businesses, and individuals recognizing their vast potential. Incentives and grants are being offered to promote the construction and retrofitting of existing buildings to achieve net-zero energy status. Moreover, advancements in technology and energy storage systems are making these buildings more efficient and affordable, further driving their widespread adoption.

As we move towards a more sustainable future, net-zero energy buildings will undoubtedly play a crucial role. By embracing these energy-efficient structures, we can strive towards a world where buildings are no longer a burden on the environment but instead serve as a catalyst for positive change. Whether you are an environmental engineering enthusiast, a homeowner, or simply someone interested in sustainable energy systems, understanding the concept of net-zero energy buildings is vital in shaping a cleaner, greener future for everyone.

Smart Grid Technologies for Buildings

In recent years, there has been a growing emphasis on the need to adopt sustainable energy systems in order to mitigate the adverse effects of climate change and reduce our dependence on fossil fuels. One crucial aspect of this transition is the integration of smart grid technologies into buildings. These technologies have the potential to revolutionize the way we consume and distribute energy, making our buildings more efficient and environmentally friendly.

Smart grid technologies refer to the application of advanced communication and control systems to the traditional electrical grid. By incorporating real-time data, analytics, and automation, these technologies enable a more efficient and reliable distribution of electricity. This is particularly important for buildings, as they account for a significant portion of energy consumption and greenhouse gas emissions.

One of the key benefits of smart grid technologies is the ability to optimize energy usage in buildings. Through the use of smart meters, sensors, and automated controls, building owners can monitor and manage their energy consumption in real-time. This allows for better energy management, reducing waste and lowering energy bills. Additionally, smart grid technologies enable demand response programs, where buildings can adjust their energy usage during peak times, helping to stabilize the electrical grid and avoid blackouts.

Furthermore, smart grid technologies facilitate the integration of renewable energy sources into buildings. Solar panels, wind turbines, and other sustainable energy systems can be seamlessly connected to the electrical grid, providing clean and renewable energy to power buildings. With smart grid technologies, excess energy generated by buildings can be stored and shared with other buildings, increasing overall energy efficiency and reducing reliance on non-renewable energy sources.

Another key feature of smart grid technologies is the ability to detect and isolate faults in the electrical grid. By constantly monitoring the grid, potential issues can be identified and addressed before they escalate, ensuring a more reliable and resilient energy supply.

In conclusion, smart grid technologies have the potential to revolutionize the way we consume and distribute energy in buildings. These technologies enable better energy optimization, integration of renewable energy sources, and a more reliable electrical grid. By adopting smart grid technologies, we can make our buildings more sustainable, reduce greenhouse gas emissions, and pave the way for a cleaner and greener future.

Chapter 9: Sustainable Energy for Transportation

Electric Vehicles and Charging Infrastructure

As we strive towards a greener and more sustainable future, one of the key areas that demand our attention is the transportation sector. Over the years, fossil fuel-powered vehicles have contributed significantly to air pollution and greenhouse gas emissions. However, there is a promising solution on the horizon – electric vehicles (EVs) and the development of a reliable charging infrastructure.

Electric vehicles offer a cleaner and more sustainable alternative to traditional internal combustion engine vehicles. By utilizing rechargeable batteries as their primary source of power, EVs produce zero tailpipe emissions. This not only helps combat air pollution but also reduces our dependence on fossil fuels, leading to a significant reduction in greenhouse gas emissions.

To support the widespread adoption of electric vehicles, the development of a robust charging infrastructure is crucial. Just as petrol stations are essential for conventional vehicles, charging stations play a similar role for EVs. These stations allow EV owners to recharge their vehicles conveniently and efficiently, thereby alleviating concerns about range anxiety and promoting their use as a practical transportation option.

The charging infrastructure for electric vehicles can be classified into three levels: Level 1, Level 2, and Level 3. Level 1 charging involves plugging the EV into a standard household outlet, providing a slow but accessible charging option. Level 2 charging utilizes higher-voltage charging stations and offers faster charging times. Level 3, also known as DC fast charging, provides the quickest recharge times, making it suitable for long-distance travel and public charging stations.

The implementation of a widespread charging infrastructure requires careful planning and coordination. This includes the installation of charging stations in public spaces, workplaces, residential areas, and along major highways. Governments and private entities must work together to ensure the availability and accessibility of charging stations, making electric vehicles a viable option for all.

Moreover, advancements in technology have led to the development of innovative charging solutions such as wireless charging and vehicle-to-grid (V2G) systems. Wireless charging eliminates the need for physical connections, allowing EVs to be charged simply by parking over a charging pad. V2G systems enable bi-directional energy flow, allowing EVs to not only consume electricity but also provide power back to the grid during peak demand periods.

Investing in electric vehicles and charging infrastructure is not only beneficial for the environment but also for the economy. It creates new job opportunities in manufacturing, installation, and maintenance of charging stations while reducing our reliance on imported fossil fuels.

In conclusion, electric vehicles and the development of a reliable charging infrastructure are pivotal in our transition towards sustainable energy systems. By embracing EVs and expanding charging infrastructure, we can significantly reduce air pollution, combat climate change, and drive economic growth. It is a collective effort that requires collaboration between governments, private entities, and individuals to ensure a greener and more sustainable future for all.

Hydrogen Fuel Cell Vehicles

In recent years, the world has witnessed a growing interest in sustainable transportation solutions. As concerns over climate change and air pollution continue to escalate, alternative fuel technologies have emerged as a promising solution to reduce greenhouse gas emissions and dependence on fossil fuels. One such technology that holds great promise for the future is hydrogen fuel cell vehicles.

Hydrogen fuel cell vehicles, also known as FCVs, are a type of electric vehicle that uses hydrogen as its primary fuel source. Unlike conventional electric vehicles that rely on rechargeable batteries, FCVs generate electricity through an electrochemical reaction between hydrogen and oxygen, producing water vapor as the only byproduct. This innovative technology offers several advantages over traditional gasoline-powered vehicles, making it an ideal choice for a sustainable future.

First and foremost, hydrogen fuel cell vehicles are environmentally friendly. They produce zero tailpipe emissions, which means they do not contribute to air pollution or greenhouse gas emissions. This characteristic makes FCVs a crucial player in the fight against climate change and the pursuit of cleaner air quality in urban areas.

Moreover, hydrogen fuel cell vehicles offer greater energy efficiency compared to internal combustion engines. While conventional vehicles waste a significant amount of energy through heat dissipation, FCVs convert nearly 60% of the energy stored in hydrogen into usable electricity, resulting in a more efficient and sustainable mode of transportation.

Additionally, hydrogen fuel cell vehicles provide a longer driving range and shorter refueling time compared to battery electric vehicles. FCVs can travel up to 300 miles on a single tank of hydrogen, eliminating range anxiety concerns commonly associated with electric vehicles. Moreover, refueling a hydrogen fuel cell vehicle takes only a few minutes, offering a convenience similar to that of traditional gasoline-powered vehicles.

However, despite its numerous advantages, the widespread adoption of hydrogen fuel cell vehicles faces certain challenges. The production and distribution of hydrogen fuel infrastructure are still in their early stages, requiring significant investments and widespread deployment to support a growing fleet of FCVs. Furthermore, the cost of producing hydrogen fuel cells remains relatively high, making FCVs more expensive compared to conventional vehicles.

As we continue to explore sustainable energy systems, hydrogen fuel cell vehicles hold tremendous promise in transforming the transportation sector. With ongoing advancements in technology and the commitment of governments, industry, and academia, we can expect hydrogen fuel cell vehicles to play a vital role in a greener and more sustainable future for all.

Biofuels and Sustainable Aviation Fuels

In recent years, there has been a growing concern about the environmental impact of the aviation industry. As air travel continues to increase, so does the amount of greenhouse gas emissions generated by aircraft engines. However, there is a solution on the horizon - biofuels and sustainable aviation fuels.

Biofuels, as the name suggests, are derived from biological sources such as plants, algae, and waste materials. They offer a promising alternative to conventional fossil fuels, as they have the potential to significantly reduce carbon dioxide (CO_2) emissions when used in aviation. By using biofuels, the aviation industry can make substantial progress towards achieving its sustainability goals.

One of the main advantages of biofuels is that they can be produced from renewable resources. Unlike fossil fuels, which are finite and contribute to climate change, biofuels can be continually replenished. This makes them a more sustainable option for the aviation sector. Additionally, biofuels can be blended with traditional jet fuel, allowing for a gradual transition towards cleaner energy sources.

Several types of biofuels have shown promising results in aviation. For example, hydroprocessed esters and fatty acids (HEFA) are derived from plant oils, animal fats, and algae. These fuels possess similar properties to traditional jet fuel and can be used in existing aircraft engines without any modifications. This ease of integration makes HEFA biofuels a viable option for immediate implementation.

Another type of biofuel gaining traction is synthetic paraffinic kerosene (SPK), which is produced through the Fischer-Tropsch process. SPK offers superior combustion properties, resulting in reduced emissions and improved fuel efficiency. Although still in the early stages of development, SPK holds great promise for the aviation industry's future sustainability.

In order to facilitate the adoption of biofuels in aviation, it is crucial to establish a sustainable supply chain. This involves investing in research and development, as well as creating policies and incentives to promote biofuel production. Additionally, collaborations between airlines, fuel suppliers, and governments are essential to drive the necessary changes.

By embracing biofuels and sustainable aviation fuels, the aviation industry can significantly reduce its carbon footprint and contribute to a more sustainable future. Environmental engineering plays a critical role in developing and implementing these technologies, ensuring that they meet stringent environmental standards while maintaining safety and efficiency in air travel.

In conclusion, biofuels and sustainable aviation fuels offer a promising solution to the environmental challenges faced by the aviation industry. With continuous advancements in technology and the support of environmental engineering professionals, the widespread adoption of these fuels can pave the way for a greener and more sustainable future in air travel.

Public Transportation and Sustainable Mobility

In today's rapidly urbanizing world, the need for sustainable mobility solutions has become more pressing than ever. With the growing concerns about climate change and air pollution, it is evident that we need to rethink our transportation systems. This subchapter explores the crucial role of public transportation in achieving sustainable mobility and its potential benefits for the environment and society.

Public transportation offers an efficient and eco-friendly alternative to private vehicles, which are a significant contributor to greenhouse gas emissions. By opting for buses, trams, trains, or subways, individuals reduce their carbon footprint and help combat climate change. Moreover, public transportation systems can accommodate a large number of passengers, reducing traffic congestion and alleviating the strain on existing road infrastructure.

One of the key advantages of public transportation is its ability to promote social equity and inclusivity. It ensures that all individuals, regardless of their income or physical abilities, have access to affordable and convenient transportation options. This inclusivity is particularly vital in urban areas where marginalized communities often face limited mobility options. By improving access to education, employment, and healthcare, public transportation contributes to a more equitable society.

Public transportation also plays a crucial role in enhancing the quality of urban life. As cities become more congested, private vehicle use leads to increased noise pollution, reduced air quality, and diminished public spaces. By prioritizing public transportation, cities can reclaim space for parks, bike lanes, and pedestrian zones, creating healthier and more vibrant communities. Additionally, public transportation promotes active and sustainable modes of transportation, such as walking and cycling, by providing first and last-mile connections.

To fully harness the potential of public transportation, it is important to invest in modernizing and expanding existing systems. Improving the reliability, frequency, and coverage of public transportation services will encourage more individuals to shift from private vehicles to sustainable modes of transportation. Furthermore, integrating emerging technologies, such as electric buses and autonomous vehicles, can significantly reduce the environmental impact of public transportation.

In conclusion, public transportation is a vital component of sustainable mobility and offers numerous benefits for both the environment and society. By prioritizing public transportation systems, we can reduce greenhouse gas emissions, enhance social equity, and improve the quality of urban life. It is crucial for governments, urban planners, and individuals to recognize the importance of public transportation in shaping a sustainable future for all.

Chapter 10: Policies and Incentives for Sustainable Energy Adoption

Government Initiatives and Regulatory Frameworks

In the pursuit of a sustainable future, it is crucial to understand the role of government initiatives and regulatory frameworks in shaping our energy systems. Governments around the world have recognized the urgent need to transition to sustainable energy sources and have taken significant steps to drive this transition forward.

One such initiative is the development of renewable energy targets. Governments have set ambitious goals to increase the share of renewable energy in their overall energy mix. These targets serve as a commitment to reduce greenhouse gas emissions and combat climate change. By encouraging the adoption of renewable energy technologies such as wind, solar, and hydroelectric power, governments are paving the way for a cleaner and more sustainable future.

To support the growth of renewable energy, governments have implemented various regulatory frameworks. These frameworks include feed-in tariffs, tax incentives, and renewable energy certificates. Feed-in tariffs provide financial incentives for individuals and businesses to generate renewable energy and sell any excess back to the grid. Tax incentives, on the other hand, offer financial benefits to those who invest in renewable energy systems. Renewable energy certificates serve as a mechanism to track and verify the generation and use of renewable energy, ensuring transparency and accountability in the energy sector.

Additionally, governments have introduced energy efficiency standards and regulations to promote the efficient use of energy resources. These standards apply to appliances, buildings, and industrial processes, aiming to reduce energy consumption and minimize waste. By enforcing energy efficiency measures, governments not only reduce greenhouse gas emissions but also help individuals and businesses save on energy costs.

Government initiatives and regulatory frameworks also play a crucial role in fostering research and development in sustainable energy technologies. Through funding programs and collaborations with universities and research institutions, governments support the innovation and commercialization of clean energy solutions. This, in turn, drives down costs and accelerates the widespread adoption of sustainable energy systems.

In conclusion, government initiatives and regulatory frameworks are vital drivers of the transition to sustainable energy systems. By setting renewable energy targets, implementing regulatory mechanisms, and promoting energy efficiency, governments pave the way for a cleaner and more sustainable future. These initiatives not only benefit the environment but also create economic opportunities and improve energy security. As individuals and professionals in the field of environmental engineering, it is crucial to stay informed and engaged with government initiatives and regulatory frameworks to contribute to the sustainable energy revolution.

Financial Incentives and Subsidies

In today's world, where the need for sustainable energy systems has become more vital than ever before, financial incentives and subsidies play a crucial role in promoting the adoption of renewable energy sources. These incentives not only encourage individuals and businesses to invest in sustainable energy systems but also make such systems more accessible and affordable for everyone.

Financial incentives and subsidies can take various forms, including tax credits, grants, rebates, and low-interest loans. These mechanisms aim to offset the initial costs of installing renewable energy systems, making them more economically viable for individuals and businesses alike. By offering financial support, governments and organizations can encourage a shift towards sustainable energy, reducing the carbon footprint and promoting a greener future.

One of the most common forms of financial incentives is a tax credit. These credits allow individuals and businesses to deduct a certain percentage of the cost of renewable energy systems from their tax liability. This not only helps to lower the overall cost of installation but also provides a tangible financial benefit for adopting sustainable energy solutions. Additionally, grants and rebates provide direct financial assistance, either by covering a portion of the installation costs or by providing a cash incentive after the system has been installed.

Low-interest loans are another effective way to promote the adoption of sustainable energy systems. These loans offer favorable terms and conditions, making it easier for individuals and businesses to finance the upfront costs of installation. By reducing the financial burden, low-interest loans make sustainable energy systems more accessible to a wider audience, including those who may have limited resources.

For the field of environmental engineering, financial incentives and subsidies are invaluable tools. They not only encourage professionals in this field to develop innovative solutions but also provide the necessary support for implementing these solutions on a larger scale. The financial incentives not only benefit environmental engineers directly but also create a ripple effect, leading to job creation, economic growth, and a healthier environment.

In conclusion, financial incentives and subsidies are essential components of sustainable energy systems. By providing support and reducing the financial burden, these mechanisms encourage the adoption of renewable energy sources, making them more accessible and affordable for everyone. With the help of financial incentives, individuals, businesses, and environmental engineering professionals can play a significant role in shaping a sustainable future for all.

International Cooperation for Sustainable Energy Transition

In today's world, the need to transition towards sustainable energy systems has become increasingly urgent. As the effects of climate change become more apparent, it is crucial for nations to come together and collaborate on finding solutions to address this global challenge. This subchapter explores the importance of international cooperation in achieving a sustainable energy transition and how it can benefit everyone, especially those in the field of environmental engineering.

The transition to sustainable energy systems requires the collective effort of nations across the globe. No single country can tackle this issue alone. By working together, countries can share knowledge, resources, and best practices to accelerate the transition process. International cooperation provides a platform for governments, researchers, and experts in the field of environmental engineering to exchange ideas, collaborate on research projects, and develop innovative technologies that can drive the sustainable energy transition.

One of the key benefits of international cooperation is the sharing of knowledge and expertise. By learning from each other's successes and failures, countries can avoid reinventing the wheel and instead focus on implementing proven strategies. For example, a country that has successfully integrated renewable energy into its grid can share its experiences and lessons learned with others, enabling them to avoid potential pitfalls and accelerate their own transition efforts.

International cooperation also fosters collaboration on research and development. By pooling resources and expertise, countries can undertake joint research projects to advance sustainable energy technologies. This collaboration can lead to breakthrough innovations and cost reductions, making sustainable energy more accessible and affordable for everyone. Moreover, international cooperation can help bridge the gap between developed and developing nations, ensuring that sustainable energy solutions are accessible to all, regardless of their economic status.

Furthermore, international cooperation facilitates the establishment of global standards and regulations. By working together, countries can harmonize their policies and regulations, creating a level playing field for sustainable energy technologies. This alignment enables the scaling up of renewable energy projects, attracts investments, and promotes the transfer of clean energy technologies to regions that need them the most.

In conclusion, international cooperation plays a vital role in achieving a sustainable energy transition. By sharing knowledge, collaborating on research, and establishing global standards, nations can collectively address the challenges of climate change and work towards a future powered by clean and renewable energy sources. For individuals in the field of environmental engineering, international cooperation offers opportunities for collaboration, learning, and innovation, ultimately contributing to a more sustainable and resilient planet for everyone.

Chapter 11: Overcoming Challenges and Ensuring a Sustainable Future

Energy Storage Technologies and Solutions

In today's world, the demand for sustainable energy systems is more crucial than ever. As we continue to search for alternatives to fossil fuels, energy storage technologies play a vital role in ensuring a reliable and efficient energy supply. This subchapter will delve into the various energy storage solutions available and their significance in the quest for a sustainable future.

One of the most promising energy storage technologies is battery storage. Batteries have come a long way in recent years, with advancements in lithium-ion and solid-state battery technologies. These batteries can store energy generated from renewable sources such as solar and wind, allowing for a continuous power supply even when the sun isn't shining or the wind isn't blowing. Battery storage systems are not only suitable for residential applications but also have the potential to revolutionize the transportation sector by powering electric vehicles.

Another energy storage solution is pumped hydro storage. This technology harnesses the power of gravity by pumping water uphill during periods of low energy demand and releasing it to generate electricity during peak demand. Pumped hydro storage facilities can store large amounts of energy and provide grid stability, making them an essential component of a sustainable energy system.

Furthermore, thermal energy storage offers a unique approach to storing energy. This technology converts excess energy into heat and stores it for later use in various applications such as heating, cooling, and industrial processes. Thermal energy storage systems can utilize materials like molten salt or phase-change materials to store and release energy efficiently.

Additionally, hydrogen storage is gaining momentum as a viable energy storage solution. Hydrogen can be produced through electrolysis, using excess renewable energy, and stored for later use in fuel cells or as a clean-burning fuel. Hydrogen storage has the potential to provide long-duration energy storage and decarbonize sectors that are challenging to electrify, such as heavy industry and long-haul transportation.

These energy storage technologies and solutions are vital for environmental engineering and the broader goal of achieving sustainable energy systems. By enabling the integration of renewable energy sources and providing grid stability, these technologies pave the way for a future powered by clean and abundant energy.

As we move forward, it is crucial for individuals, policymakers, and industries to understand the significance of energy storage and actively support its development and implementation. By investing in research, innovation, and infrastructure, we can unlock the full potential of energy storage technologies and transition towards a greener and more sustainable future for everyone.

Grid Modernization and Resilience

In today's rapidly evolving world, the need for sustainable energy systems has become paramount. As we strive to create a greener and cleaner future, one of the key areas that demand our attention is grid modernization and resilience. This subchapter aims to shed light on the significance of grid modernization and resilience in the context of sustainable energy systems, particularly for those interested in environmental engineering.

Grid modernization refers to the process of upgrading and transforming the traditional power grid into a smart, efficient, and decentralized network. The traditional grid, which relies heavily on fossil fuels, is not only inefficient but also vulnerable to disruptions and outages. With the integration of modern technologies, such as advanced sensors, communication systems, and data analytics, the grid can become more reliable, flexible, and sustainable.

One of the primary goals of grid modernization is to enable the seamless integration of renewable energy sources, such as solar and wind, into the grid. By doing so, we can reduce our reliance on fossil fuels and mitigate the adverse environmental impacts associated with traditional energy generation. Additionally, a modernized grid can facilitate the widespread adoption of electric vehicles, energy storage systems, and demand response programs, further enhancing the sustainability and efficiency of our energy systems.

Resilience is another crucial aspect of grid modernization. As climate change continues to pose significant challenges, including extreme weather events and natural disasters, our energy systems must be able to withstand and recover from these disruptions. By incorporating resilience measures into the grid, such as microgrids, backup power systems, and improved infrastructure, we can ensure a more reliable and resilient energy supply, even in the face of adversity.

For environmental engineering professionals, understanding the intricacies of grid modernization and resilience is essential. It equips them with the knowledge and skills required to design and implement sustainable energy systems that can withstand the challenges of the future. By incorporating these concepts into their work, environmental engineers can contribute to building a more resilient, efficient, and environmentally friendly energy infrastructure.

In conclusion, grid modernization and resilience are critical components of sustainable energy systems. By upgrading and transforming the traditional grid, we can create a more reliable, efficient, and sustainable energy infrastructure. For environmental engineering professionals and anyone interested in sustainable energy, understanding these concepts is crucial in driving the transition towards a greener and cleaner future.

Energy Education and Awareness

In today's fast-paced world, energy is an essential part of our daily lives. We rely on it to power our homes, businesses, and transportation systems. However, with the increasing demand for energy, it is more important than ever to educate ourselves about sustainable energy systems and raise awareness about their benefits. This subchapter aims to provide a comprehensive understanding of energy education and awareness for individuals from all walks of life, with a particular focus on those interested in environmental engineering.

Energy education is the foundation upon which a sustainable future is built. It equips us with the knowledge and tools needed to make informed decisions about energy consumption, conservation, and renewable energy sources. By understanding the environmental impact of different energy systems, we can actively contribute to reducing greenhouse gas emissions and combating climate change.

Awareness about sustainable energy is crucial for everyone, as it encourages individuals to take action that benefits both the planet and their own well-being. This subchapter will delve into various aspects of energy education and awareness, including the science behind energy production, the importance of energy conservation, and the benefits of renewable energy sources.

Environmental engineering professionals play a pivotal role in shaping a sustainable future. This subchapter will specifically cater to their interests by exploring the latest advancements in energy technology, sustainable infrastructure development, and policy frameworks. It will also touch upon the interdisciplinary nature of environmental engineering, emphasizing the need for collaboration with other fields to address complex energy challenges.

Moreover, this subchapter will highlight successful case studies of sustainable energy projects from around the world. These examples will showcase the potential of renewable energy sources, such as solar, wind, and hydropower, to transform communities and industries. By understanding these real-world examples, environmental engineering professionals can gain insights into the practical implementation of sustainable energy systems.

Whether you are an environmental engineering professional or simply someone interested in sustainable energy, this subchapter will provide valuable insights into the world of energy education and awareness. By empowering individuals with knowledge and fostering a sense of responsibility, we can collectively work towards a future powered by clean and renewable energy. Let us embark on this journey together and become catalysts for change in the sustainable energy landscape.

Collaborative Efforts for Sustainable Energy Development

Introduction:

In today's rapidly changing world, the need for sustainable energy development has become more critical than ever. As we strive towards a greener future, collaborative efforts play a pivotal role in shaping the path towards sustainable energy systems. This subchapter will explore the importance of collaboration in the context of sustainable energy development, addressing the audience of "everyone" and specifically focusing on the niche of Environmental Engineering.

1. The Power of Collaboration: Collaborative efforts bring together diverse perspectives and expertise, creating a synergy that can drive significant progress in sustainable energy development. By pooling resources, knowledge, and skills, individuals, organizations, and governments can tackle complex challenges more effectively. Environmental engineers, with their deep understanding of environmental systems, play a crucial role in collaborating with other stakeholders to develop sustainable energy solutions.

2. Public-Private Partnerships: One effective form of collaboration is the establishment of public-private partnerships. By joining forces, governments and private companies can leverage their respective strengths to accelerate the transition towards sustainable energy. Such partnerships can facilitate the funding, research, and development of innovative technologies, as well as the implementation of large-scale renewable energy projects, benefiting both the economy and the environment.

3. Knowledge Sharing and Capacity Building: Collaboration also involves sharing knowledge and building capacity

within the field of environmental engineering. Through conferences, workshops, and research collaborations, professionals can exchange best practices, learn from each other's experiences, and stay updated on the latest advancements in sustainable energy systems. This collective learning fosters an environment of continuous improvement and drives innovation in the field.

4. International Cooperation:
Global challenges require global solutions. International cooperation is essential for sustainable energy development, as it allows countries to learn from each other, share resources, and harmonize policies and regulations. Collaborative initiatives such as the Paris Agreement provide a platform for countries to work together towards common goals, promoting the adoption of renewable energy sources and reducing greenhouse gas emissions on a global scale.

5. Community Engagement:
Collaborative efforts should extend beyond government and industry partnerships to include local communities. Environmental engineers can play a vital role in engaging communities, raising awareness about sustainable energy options, and involving them in decision-making processes. By building trust and empowering communities, sustainable energy projects can be developed in a manner that aligns with their specific needs and values.

Conclusion:
Collaborative efforts are crucial in achieving sustainable energy development. By fostering partnerships, sharing knowledge, promoting international cooperation, and engaging communities, environmental engineers and other stakeholders can drive the transition towards a more sustainable and resilient energy future.

Together, we can power the future and create a world where sustainable energy systems benefit everyone.

Chapter 12: The Role of Individuals in Powering the Future

Energy Conservation and Efficiency Measures

In the quest for a sustainable future, it is imperative that we understand and implement energy conservation and efficiency measures. This subchapter aims to provide a comprehensive guide to individuals, including those in the field of environmental engineering, on how to effectively conserve energy and enhance efficiency in various aspects of their lives.

Energy conservation refers to the practice of using energy efficiently and reducing unnecessary energy consumption. It involves making conscious choices to limit energy usage, such as turning off lights when not in use, utilizing natural light during the day, and adjusting thermostats to optimal temperatures. By adopting simple habits like these, we can significantly reduce our energy consumption and make a positive impact on the environment.

Efficiency measures, on the other hand, focus on maximizing the output of energy while minimizing input. This can be achieved by using energy-efficient appliances, such as LED light bulbs and energy-star rated electronics, which consume less energy than their conventional counterparts. Additionally, optimizing building designs to incorporate proper insulation, efficient heating and cooling systems, and utilizing renewable energy sources like solar panels can greatly improve energy efficiency.

Transportation is another crucial area where energy conservation and efficiency measures should be implemented. Choosing fuel-efficient vehicles, carpooling, and using public transportation are effective ways to reduce energy consumption and greenhouse gas emissions. Moreover, adopting alternative modes of transportation like cycling or walking for short distances not only conserves energy but also promotes a healthier lifestyle.

In the industrial sector, businesses can implement energy audits to identify areas of energy wastage and develop strategies to minimize it. Upgrading machinery and equipment to more energy-efficient models, optimizing production processes, and incorporating energy management systems can result in significant energy savings. By embracing sustainable practices, businesses can not only reduce their environmental footprint but also enhance their profitability in the long run.

It is essential for individuals, environmental engineers, and other stakeholders to raise awareness about energy conservation and efficiency. Education and outreach programs can play a vital role in encouraging people to adopt energy-saving habits and promoting the benefits of sustainable energy systems. By working together, we can create a future where energy conservation and efficiency are integral parts of our daily lives, ensuring a more sustainable and environmentally friendly world for everyone.

In conclusion, energy conservation and efficiency measures are vital for achieving a sustainable energy future. By adopting simple yet effective strategies in our homes, transportation, and industries, we can significantly reduce energy consumption and minimize our impact on the environment. It is a collective responsibility of every individual, including those in the field of environmental engineering, to educate and promote energy conservation to create a greener and more sustainable world for ourselves and future generations.

Consumer Choices for Sustainable Energy

In today's rapidly changing world, the need for sustainable energy solutions has become more critical than ever. As the impacts of climate change become increasingly evident, individuals and communities are seeking ways to reduce their carbon footprint and transition to a cleaner and more sustainable energy future. This subchapter, titled "Consumer Choices for Sustainable Energy," aims to guide readers – from all walks of life, including those interested in environmental engineering – on making informed decisions that contribute to a more sustainable energy system.

Consumer choices play a significant role in shaping the energy landscape. By making conscious decisions, individuals can have a direct impact on reducing greenhouse gas emissions, enhancing energy efficiency, and promoting the use of renewable resources. This subchapter focuses on empowering readers to make sustainable energy choices that align with their values and environmental goals.

The first section of this subchapter provides an overview of sustainable energy sources, such as solar, wind, hydropower, geothermal, and bioenergy. It delves into the advantages and limitations of each source, helping readers understand the potential of renewable energy technologies in meeting their energy needs. By presenting case studies and success stories from around the world, readers can gain inspiration and insight into the practical implementation of sustainable energy solutions.

The second section explores consumer choices in the context of energy efficiency. It highlights the importance of energy conservation and presents a range of energy-efficient options for residential, commercial, and industrial sectors. From energy-efficient appliances to smart home technologies, readers will discover practical ways to reduce energy consumption and save money while contributing to a more sustainable future.

The final section of this subchapter delves into the concept of green purchasing and renewable energy certificates. It explains how individuals can support the development of renewable energy projects by purchasing renewable energy credits and participating in community solar programs. Additionally, readers will learn about the importance of considering the lifecycle impacts of their consumer choices and how to make sustainable decisions beyond just energy sources.

Ultimately, this subchapter aims to empower readers to become active participants in the transition towards sustainable energy systems. By understanding the choices available and their potential impact, individuals can make informed decisions that align with their values and contribute to a healthier and more sustainable planet. Whether you are an environmental engineering enthusiast or simply someone interested in making a difference, this subchapter will provide you with the knowledge and tools needed to navigate the world of sustainable energy choices.

Community-Based Energy Projects

In recent years, there has been a growing interest in community-based energy projects as a means to address the environmental challenges we face and create a more sustainable future. These projects involve the active participation of local communities in the generation, distribution, and consumption of renewable energy. By empowering individuals and communities to take charge of their energy needs, community-based energy projects have the potential to transform the way we produce and consume energy.

One of the key benefits of community-based energy projects is their positive environmental impact. By harnessing renewable energy sources such as solar, wind, and hydro, these projects reduce our reliance on fossil fuels and decrease greenhouse gas emissions. This shift towards clean energy not only helps combat climate change but also improves air quality and reduces health risks associated with traditional energy sources.

Moreover, community-based energy projects provide economic benefits to the communities involved. By investing in local renewable energy infrastructure, communities can create jobs and stimulate economic growth. These projects also promote energy independence, as communities become less dependent on external sources of energy and more self-sufficient. This energy self-sufficiency can reduce the vulnerability of communities to fluctuations in energy prices and supply disruptions.

Community-based energy projects also foster social cohesion and empowerment within communities. By involving community members in decision-making processes and allowing them to benefit from the generated energy, these projects create a sense of ownership and pride. Additionally, they educate individuals about energy conservation and promote sustainable lifestyles, leading to a more environmentally conscious population.

Implementing community-based energy projects does come with challenges. One of the main obstacles is securing the necessary funding and resources. However, various funding options, including government grants, community crowdfunding, and cooperative models, can be explored to overcome this hurdle. Furthermore, navigating regulatory frameworks and ensuring community engagement and participation can be complex but are crucial for the success of these projects.

In conclusion, community-based energy projects have emerged as a promising solution to our energy and environmental challenges. They empower communities to take control of their energy future, promote sustainability, and bring economic and social benefits. By investing in renewable energy infrastructure at the local level, communities can contribute to a more sustainable and resilient energy system for everyone. As individuals and as a society, it is our responsibility to support and participate in these projects to ensure a brighter and greener future for generations to come.

Empowering Individuals to Drive Change

In today's world, the need for sustainable energy systems has become increasingly important. As we face the challenges of climate change and dwindling natural resources, it is crucial that we empower individuals to drive change towards a more sustainable future. This subchapter aims to inspire and provide practical guidance to everyone, with a particular focus on the niches of environmental engineering.

One of the key aspects of empowering individuals to drive change is education and awareness. It is essential for everyone to understand the importance of sustainable energy and its impact on our environment. By educating ourselves and others on the benefits of renewable energy sources like solar, wind, and hydroelectric power, we can make informed decisions and take action towards a greener future. Environmental engineering professionals play a vital role in this process by spreading knowledge and developing innovative solutions.

Another crucial aspect of empowerment is providing access to sustainable energy technologies. Many individuals may be willing to adopt renewable energy systems but lack the resources or knowledge to do so. By making sustainable energy technologies more accessible and affordable, we can empower individuals to take control of their energy consumption. This can be achieved through government initiatives, financial incentives, and community-driven projects supported by environmental engineers.

In addition to education and accessibility, collaboration and community engagement are crucial for empowering individuals. Sustainable energy systems require collective effort and cooperation. By fostering a sense of community and encouraging collaboration, individuals can come together to implement sustainable energy solutions at a local level. Environmental engineering professionals can facilitate this process by organizing workshops, seminars, and community projects that promote sustainable energy practices.

Empowering individuals to drive change also involves encouraging innovation and entrepreneurship. Sustainable energy systems require continuous improvement and new ideas. By fostering an environment that supports innovation and entrepreneurial spirit, individuals can develop and implement groundbreaking solutions to our energy challenges. Environmental engineering professionals can mentor aspiring entrepreneurs and provide valuable guidance to help transform innovative ideas into practical reality.

In conclusion, empowering individuals to drive change towards sustainable energy systems is essential for a greener and more sustainable future. By educating, providing access, fostering collaboration, and encouraging innovation, we can create a collective movement towards a more sustainable world. This subchapter aims to inspire and guide everyone, particularly those in the field of environmental engineering, to take up the mantle and become agents of change in the journey towards a sustainable energy future. Together, we can make a difference and power the future for generations to come.

Conclusion: Embracing Sustainable Energy Systems for a Brighter Future

In today's world, the need to shift towards sustainable energy systems has become more crucial than ever before. As we face the challenges of climate change and depleting fossil fuel resources, it is evident that embracing sustainable energy is the key to ensuring a brighter future for our planet. This conclusion aims to summarize the importance of sustainable energy systems and their potential benefits, particularly for the audience of "everyone" and the niche of environmental engineering.

Sustainable energy systems offer a multitude of advantages. First and foremost, they significantly reduce our carbon footprint by minimizing greenhouse gas emissions. By transitioning from fossil fuels to renewable energy sources like solar, wind, hydro, and geothermal, we can mitigate the impacts of climate change and work towards achieving global sustainability goals. These systems also decrease our dependence on finite resources, ensuring a more secure and reliable energy supply for future generations.

For the audience of "everyone," embracing sustainable energy systems provides numerous benefits on an individual level as well. By installing solar panels on rooftops or using energy-efficient appliances, we can reduce our energy bills, saving money in the long run. Furthermore, sustainable energy systems foster job creation and economic growth, as the renewable energy sector continues to expand. This provides opportunities for individuals to not only contribute to a greener future but also participate in a thriving industry.

Within the niche of environmental engineering, the importance of sustainable energy systems cannot be overstated. Environmental engineers play a pivotal role in designing, implementing, and managing these systems to ensure their optimal performance and minimize environmental impacts. By harnessing their expertise, environmental engineers can steer society towards a more sustainable path, promoting the development of innovative technologies and policies.

In conclusion, the transition towards sustainable energy systems is imperative for a brighter future. It is a collective responsibility that requires the participation of "everyone" to ensure the preservation of our planet for future generations. The benefits of embracing sustainable energy systems extend beyond environmental considerations, encompassing economic, social, and individual advantages. For environmental engineers, this shift presents an opportunity to utilize their skills and knowledge to drive change and make a lasting impact. By embracing sustainable energy systems, we can forge a path towards a cleaner, healthier, and more sustainable future for all. Together, let us power the future and create a world that thrives on renewable energy.

www.ingramcontent.com/pod-product-compliance
Lightning Source LLC
LaVergne TN
LVHW051954060526
838201LV00059B/3648